IRISH MISCELLANY

EVERYTHING YOU ALWAYS WANTED TO KNOW ABOUT IRELAND

BY

DERMOT MCEVOY

Skyhorse Publishing

Skyhorse Publishing books may be purchased in bulk at special discounts for sales promotion, corporate gifts, fund-raising, or educational purposes. Special editions can also be created to specifications. For details, contact the Special Sales Department, Skyhorse Publishing, 307 West 36th Street, 11th Floor, New York, NY 10018 or info@skyhorsepublishing.com.

Skyhorse® and Skyhorse Publishing® are registered trademarks of Skyhorse Publishing, Inc.®, a Delaware corporation.

Visit our website at www.skyhorsepublishing.com.

10 9 8 7 6 5 4 3 2 1

Library of Congress Cataloging-in-Publication Data is available on file.

Cover design by Adam Bozarth
Cover photo credit Thinkstock

Print ISBN: 978-1-62914-516-7
Ebook ISBN: 978-1-63220-009-9

Printed in China

This book is dedicated to
Marianne Fagan—critic, fan, friend.
Thank you.

TABLE OF CONTENTS

INTRODUCTION

What makes the Irish, well, Irish? It is the billion dollar question, and it has no simple answer.

There are hundreds of things—some prominent, most mundane, some cloaked in secrecy, most deservedly obscure—that coalesce to make a race: language, climate, religion, the land, song, food, laughter, poverty, diaspora, famine, revolution.

To the outside world—and that would include the American Irish—there are several stereotypes attached to the Irish. These stereotypes can be swiftly called to mind: Catholic, drinkers, fighters, revolutionaries, terrorists, writers, superstitious, Gaelic, pious, extravagant—just to name a few. You'll see caricatures around the time of St. Patrick's Day with green hats and green beer, like it's a joke. But famine and diaspora and revolution are no joke. A toughness was burned into this race that is impossible to shake.

Like many stereotypes, there is a grain of truth in all of them. But stereotypes can be tricky, especially Irish ones. Yes, Ireland is a Catholic country, but the Irish also have a rich cultural and political tradition bestowed on them by their fellow Protestant and Jewish brothers. They are drinkers, but they also have a disproportionate amount of Pioneers, severe teetotalers. They will fight for their own freedom and rights but are also an important part of United Nation peacekeeping missions in far-off corners of the globe. To know—to understand—the Irish, one must look through their history and their culture to understand how this sturdy, implausible race survived, not only in Ireland, but around the world.

So look inside and find some of the miscellany that makes the Irish, well, Irish. It's not all pretty, and sometimes it's downright ugly, but through and through it's impossibly colorful and edifying and, of course, very Irish.

1

HOW'S YOUR ERSE?
ADVENTURES IN THE IRISH
LANGUAGE

If someone in Ireland asks you "How's your Erse?" they are not inquiring about the health of your buttocks. (Note: the preferred Irish designation for the *derrière* is "arse.")

"Erse" is what they call Irish Gaelic.

There are two official languages in the Republic of Ireland—English and Irish—a language also known as Gaelic, especially by Americans. (There are three Gaelic languages: Irish, Scotch, and Manx; Irish is the most prominent.) Irish is spoken mostly in the west of the country and in the *Gaeltacht*, or Irish-speaking enclaves.

Although English is the majority language, Irish is used frequently, with an estimated 5 to 10 percent of the population using it as their primary language. There are Irish-speaking channels on television and radio and such things as street and road signs are bilingual. The Irish national anthem, *Amhrán na bhFiann* ("The Soldier's Song"), is always sung in Irish. So Irish words are used fluently and effectively. While visiting Ireland you may come in contact with some of these frequently used Irish words:

Pleasantries	
Dia Duit	hello
Fáilte	welcome
Cead mile fáilte	one hundred thousand welcomes (a typical Irish greeting)
Go raibh maith agat	thank you
Sláinte	health (a common Irish toast)
Slán	goodbye

Places/Travel

Éire	Ireland; the official name of Ireland
Poblacht na hÉireann	the Republic of Ireland
Oifig an Phoist	post office
An Lar	The Centre, as in City Centre, often seen in bus destination boxes
Baile Átha Cliath	Dublin, or "the town of the hurdled ford," often seen on buses
Aer Lingus	air boats or air fleet, Ireland's national airline
Bóthar	road

Food

Bia	food
Bricfeasta	breakfast
Tae	tea
Caifé	coffee
Bainne	milk
Siúcra	sugar
Uisce	water
Uisce beatha	the "water of life," corrupted by the English into "whiskey"

Government

Taoiseach	Irish word for leader or chief, i.e., the Irish prime minister
Tánaiste	deputy prime minister
An Uachtaráin	Irish president

Áras an Uachtaráin	"The President's House," the official residence of the President of Ireland in Dublin's Phoenix Park
Dáil Éireann	Irish parliament
Garda Síochána	"Civic Guards," Irish national police force, referred to as "the Guards"
Gaeilge	Irish
Béarla	English
Raidió Teilifís Éireann	RTE, Ireland's national radio and television network

Common Words	
Leithreas	toilet; know your *fir* (men) from your *mna* (women)
Tacsaí	taxi
Stad	stop
Ceol	music
Leabhar	book
Madra	dog
Capall	horse
Sásta	happy or satisfied
Brón	sad
Fliuch	wet, as in the weather
Nuacht	news
Go maith	good
Craic	fun, often used as in "that was great *craic* last night"
Grá	love
Cailín	girl
Buachaill	boy
Garsún	young boy
Scoil	school, as in school bus

And the final transition from Erse to Arse: *Póg mo thóin* — Kiss my arse!

2

UNDERSTANDING IRISH SLANG: DON'T GET SLAGGED BECAUSE YOU'RE AN EEJIT

When I was a little boy, my father, when he was proud of me, would often proclaim, "He's my *garsún!*" When he was not so proud of me, he would shout, "You fookin' eejit!"

As previously noted, *garsún* is the Irish for a young boy. Eejit, on the other hand, is an English word that is wrapped in Irishness. It means "fool" or "idiot" and it would seem to derive, in some way, from idiot. But it is very Irish. If you drink too much and make a fool of yourself at the pub, you're an eejit. If you forget to turn on the oven to bake the roast, then you're also an eejit.

The Irish have many words that mystify Americans. You can overhear a conversation in a pub and be clueless to what's being spoken about. Here are a few words that may help you.

Arseways—to mess up; "arse" is, of course, the favorite Irish phrase for ass or buttocks

Chiseler—Dublin slang for a child

Cod/Coddin'/All-the-Cod—pulling somebody's leg

Culchie—Dubliner's term for a country person

Cute 'hoor—phrase for a self-serving person

Donkey's Years—a long time

Dublin 4/D4—the postal code for one of the fanciest neighborhoods in Dublin

Eff off—fuck off; "F" is often used instead of fuck

Fag—a cigarette; usually not used as a derisive term for a homosexual

Feck off—go away; close to "eff off"

Fenian—an elite, albeit usually unsuccessful, Irish revolutionary; it is a highly regarded term when used by Nationalists and a negative epithet when employed by Unionists

Football—what the Irish call soccer

Gander—a quick glance

Gaol—jail or prison

Gas—very funny

Give out—reprimand someone

Gobshite—a useless person; "gob" is slang for mouth and "shite" is, as someone once said in jest, the Irish past tense for shit

Gombeen Man—a money lender; always a despised figure

Lough Derg is the second largest lake in Ireland.

Gouger—an aggressive male, sort of the male counterpart of the American phrase "cougar"

Holy Joe—a sanctimonious individual

Hoolie—an Irish party

'Hoor—whore

Jackeen—a Dublin person; often used disparagingly by culchies

Jacks/Jiggs—the bathroom

The Joy—Mountjoy Gaol in Dublin

Kip—a place to sleep; Dublin's red light district was often called "The Kips"

Knackered—exhausted

Lash—to rain heavily, as in "it's lashing outside"

Lough—a lake

Ossified or stocious—drunk

Peat—dead vegetation found in a bog used by the Irish as fuel instead of wood or coal (Joke: What do you call a 200-year-old Irishman? Peat!)

Poteen—illegal whiskey, i.e., Irish moonshine

Shebeen—an illegal pub, i.e., a speakeasy

Slag—a gentle put-down

Souper—one who "who took the [Protestant] soup" during the famine in exchange for the abandonment of their Catholic religion; i.e., a traitor

Stone—a measurement of 14 pounds: "Your man weighs 10 stone."

Thick—stupid; Samuel Beckett was once told that his students at Trinity were "the cream of the crop of Irish society." "Yes," he replied, "rich and thick."

Turf Accountant—a bookmaker

Wee—small or tiny

Yoke—a thing, as in "what's that yoke for?"

Your Man/Your Woman—a third person referral to the person you're talking about

3

NAME THAT IRISH PEJORATIVE

I am always amazed when Irish Americans attack America's new immigrants. Without any sense of irony—I guess their ancestors came over business class on the coffin ships—these pillars of the establishment, many of them in the media, like to toss around phrases like "anchor babies," "wetbacks," and "illegals" as if *their* DNA had some kind of divine right to American citizenship. Little have they learned from the experiences of the Irish when they were the minority.

There were all kinds of epithets aimed at the Irish. One of the favorites was referring to them as "harps," obviously after the national musical instrument of Ireland; today it is the official symbol of both the Irish government and the Guinness Brewery. (In fact, Irish-American novelist John Gregory Dunne wrote a wonderful book about his family, and he called it *Harp*.)

First names were also great fodder. The Irishman was a "Mick" (short for Michael) or "Paddy" (Patrick). And, of course, you will still hear to this day when a police prison van goes by: "There goes a paddy wagon!" Whenever I hear paddy wagon I take it as a badge of honor, thinking how hard the Irish worked for that degenerate sobriquet.

Some Irish as a badge of honor among themselves, will often refer to themselves as harps, micks, or paddies. They will also throw in a few well-used "donkeys"—obviously bestowed on the Irish by American WASPs because of the well-documented obstinacy of their Celtic brothers.

Apparently the Irish need to fight had a lot to do with some of their nicknames. (Cartoonist Thomas Nast would make a career out of portraying fighting micks.) "Hooligan" was taken from an Irish surname because of the rowdiness of said Irish family. I remember as a child New York Mets Hall of Fame broadcaster Bob Murphy referring to a fight on the ball field as a "Pier 17 Donnybrook," obviously named after the Dublin suburb where they must have had a few interesting Saturday nights.

Of course, the Protestants of Northern Ireland also had terms of endearment for their Catholic minority neighbors. "Taig" is a derogatory term that connects nationalistic instincts to its Catholic target. Like "Mick" and "Paddy," it derives from "Tadhg," the Irish for Timothy.

The Black North (Northern Ireland, that is) has also given us "RCs" for "rat catchers," a not-so-subtle code for Roman Catholics. RCs then morphed to "terriers" because said breed were thought to be the best rat catchers in contests held in the holds of grain ships in Belfast Lough.

And sometimes—unlike rat catchers and Taigs—the pejorative wasn't as politically correct. Take, for instance, "Pug-nosed Bogtrotters." I'll leave the origin of that one up to your imagination.

4

PROTESTANTS OF THE
REPUBLIC, TAKE A BOW

The Republic of Ireland is thought worldwide to be a Catholic country, and it is true in that 84 percent of Irish citizens identified themselves as Catholic in the 2011 census. In the same census, only 3 percent of citizens described themselves as Protestant. The Protestant presence in the Republic is a given. Despite Brendan Behan's priceless definition of the Anglo-Irish—"A Protestant on a horse"—the Protestants of Ireland have had a disproportionly immense influence on the nation's cultural and political progress. Going as far back as the eighteenth century, the poor of Ireland—overwhelmingly Roman Catholic—have been defended by their Protestant countrymen.

Jonathan Swift

Perhaps the first stinging indictment of the British treatment of the Catholic population was in 1729 by Jonathan Swift, Dean of St. Patrick's Cathedral in Dublin. Today Swift is probably best known for *Gulliver's Travels*, but it is for his essay, *A Modest Proposal,* that Swift is burnt into the patriotic fabric of the Irish nation. The full title for *A Modest Proposal* takes an impossible twenty-eight words—*A Modest Proposal for Preventing the Children of Poor People in Ireland Being a Burden on Their Parents or Country, and for Making Them Beneficial to the Publick*—but it is one of the greatest, most devastating satires ever rendered on the occupiers of a nation.

A Modest Proposal offers simple ways of feeding the starving masses of Ireland: "A young healthy child well nursed, is, at a year old, a most delicious nourishing and wholesome food, whether stewed, roasted, baked, or boiled; and I make no doubt that it will equally serve in a fricassee, or a ragout." He goes on to filet Ireland's landlords: "I grant this food may be somewhat dear, and therefore very proper for Landlords, who as they have already devoured most of the Parents, seem to have the best Title to the Children." And not content to stop at the landlords, Swift takes sharper aim: "For this kind of commodity will not bear exportation, and flesh being of too tender a consistence, to admit a long continuance in salt, although perhaps I could name a country, which would be glad to eat up our whole nation without it."

Now what "country" could the good Dean being thinking of?

The Society of United Irishmen

It seems that revolution is part of the Irish DNA. The first "modern" Irish rebellion occurred in 1798. This insurrection was led by the Society of United Irishmen, a group of well-educated Protestants (mostly Presbyterians), much influenced by the American and French revolutions. Their names are firmly planted in Irish revolutionary lore; prominent among them are Theobald Wolfe Tone, Robert Emmet, Lord Edward FitzGerald, and the Sheares Brothers.

As far back as 1791, Wolfe Tone published *An Argument on Behalf of the Catholics of Ireland*. The United Irishmen soon concluded what was wrong with Ireland: "We have no national government; we are ruled by Englishmen, and thus servants of Englishmen, whose object is the interest of another country, whose instrument is corruption; whose strength is the weakness of Ireland."

Wolfe Tone Statue, St. Stephen's Green, Dublin

Forced underground, the United Irishmen (some 280,000 men strong) started plotting revolution for 1798, which would become known as "The Year of the French." Unfortunately, the French showed up too late and with too few troops. The rebellion ended in utter defeat, as the Irish, many armed only with pikes, fell before British cannon, most famously at Vinegar Hill in County Wexford. Wolfe Tone defiantly declared: "From my earliest youth I have regarded the connection between Ireland and Great Britain as the curse of the Irish nation, and felt convinced that while it lasted, this country would never be free or happy. In consequence, I determined to apply all the powers which my individual efforts could move, in order to separate the two countries." He would cheat the British rope by committing suicide.

Betrayed by informers, fellow United Irishman Lord Edward FitzGerald would be captured in Dublin where he would die from his wounds. The Sheares Brothers, Henry and John, betrayed by multiple spies, were captured, executed, then drawn and quartered in Dublin. They are buried in St. Michan's Church on Church Street, famous for its mummified bodies, including the Dublin Crusader. (It is said that the Sheareses' corpses remained in perfect condition until the centennial of their death when admirers brought flowers and the moisture contained therein caused their bodies to decay. You can visit the Sheareses' coffins on tours of the crypt.) Jane "Speranza" Wilde, the mother of Oscar Wilde, remembered the perfectly preserved Sheareses in her poem "The Brothers":

Years have passed since that fatal scene of dying,
  Yet, lifelike to this day,
In their coffins still those severed heads are lying,
  Kept by angels from decay.
Oh! they preach to us, those still and pallid features—
  Those pale lips yet implore us, from their graves,
To strive for our birthright as God's creatures,
  Or die, if we can but live as slaves.

But the United Irishmen did not die with the Rebellion of 1798. In 1803 Robert Emmet organized a rebellion that failed to fully materialize. He was captured, but before he was hanged, drawn, and quartered in Dublin's Thomas Street, he gave his famous speech from the dock: "Let No Man Write My Epitaph." There is also an American connection to Emmet. His brother, Thomas Addis Emmet, also a United Irishman, finally settled in New York and became New York State's Attorney General in 1812. He is buried in the church-yard at St. Mark's in-the-Bowery in New York City's East Village.

The Young Irelanders

As time went on and Catholics secured more rights — mostly due to the emancipation efforts of Daniel "The Liberator" O'Connell — they became more involved in their own politics. But the next revo-lutionary movement — the Young Irelanders — was still headed by a Protestant, William Smith O'Brien. Actually, the revolution of 1848 was little more than a skirmish in Ballingarry, County Tipperary. For his troubles, Smith O'Brien ended up in a penal colony in Australia where he joined another, more militant Protestant Young Irelander, John Mitchel.

Mitchel, a prolific journalist, is one of the great contradictions of Irish history. A stalwart for Irish freedom, he became an apolo-gist for slavery after he settled in the United States before the American Civil War. He considered slaves "an innately inferior people." He also described President Lincoln as "an ignoramus and a boor." His *Jail Journal* is still studied to this day.

Robert Emmet

The Uncrowned King of Ireland

As more and more Catholics went into politics and were elected to the British parlia-ment in Westminster, they still found their leader to be Protestant—the charismatic Charles Stewart Parnell. First elected to parliament in 1875, Parnell cultivated many of the Fenian hierarchy (he may or may not have been a member of the Irish Republican Brotherhood [IRB], but he was more politician than revolutionary anyway) before becoming leader of the Irish Nationalist Land League in 1879. Parnell took a militant stand, warning tenants that they "must show the landlord that you intend to keep a firm grip on your homesteads and lands. You must not allow yourselves be dispossessed as you were dispossessed in 1847."

Parnell's agitating landed him in Kilmainham Gaol under the Protection of Person and Property Act of 1881—known more popularly in Ireland as the Coercion Act—which allowed imprisonment without trial, a tactic the British would enact again and again up through their Northern Ireland fiascos in the latter part of the twentieth century.

Released from prison, Parnell organized the Irish Parliamentary Party (IPP), which played a pivotal part in the failed Home Rule Bill of 1885. He was at the height of his powers when he was caught in an adulterous scandal with Kitty O'Shea. The affair had been a long one and Parnell had fathered three of Mrs. O'Shea's children. (Captain O'Shea, Kitty's husband, was a colleague of Parnell, knew of the long affair, and put off the divorce while waiting for an inheritance from his wife. He comes across as a manipulative, knowing cuckold with a bit of knucklehead thrown in for good measure.) Catholic Ireland, of course, was appalled, and Parnell was deserted by longtime friends and supporters. Broken, the "Uncrowned King of Ireland" died on October 6, 1891.

Protestant Fenian Women

I have not forgotten about the tough Fenian women who helped create the modern Irish state. Their names are legendary: the Countess Markievicz, Maud Gonne, Kathleen Clarke, Grace Gifford Plunkett, and—of all people—Lord French's sister, Charlotte Despard. For more about them and others, check out Chapter 7: "Ferocious Fenian Women."

Cornering the Nobel Market

Not all of Ireland's prominent Protestants were agitators, revolutionaries, and politicians.

If Ireland is known for anything, it is probably the disproportionate number of world-class writers it has produced compared to its small population. Four Irishmen have won the Nobel Prize in Literature: William Butler Yeats (1923), George Bernard Shaw (1925), Samuel Beckett (1969), and Séamus Heaney (1995). All of them, except Heaney, are Protestant. And, in their own way, many

W.B. Yeats

of these exceptional writers have fought for Ireland.

Yeats's play, *Cathleen Ni Houlihan* (some say cowritten by Lady Gregory), premiered on opening night of the Abbey Theatre in 1904. The play takes place during the Rising of '98 and the heroine of the title represents the Irish nation. It is fiercely nationalistic and encourages armed rebellion. Years later Yeats would write: *"Did that play of mine send out/Certain men the English shot?"* After the 1916 Easter Rising he would immortalize the events and the players in such poems as "Easter 1916," "Sixteen Dead Men," "The Rose Tree," and "The Ghost of Roger Casement." After winning the Nobel, Yeats would serve his newly independent country as a senator.

Shaw was a tough nationalist in his own right. As the British were preparing to hang Sir Roger Casement, the last rebel of the 1916 Rebellion, Shaw fought to save him—to no avail. The British would have their sixteenth martyr. He later became a friend of fiery revolutionary Michael Collins and would dine with him on the last weekend of Collins's life. After his death, Shaw would exuberantly write to Collins's sister: "I rejoice in his memory, and will not be so disloyal to it as to snivel over his valiant death. So tear up your mourning and hang up your brightest colours in his honour; and let us all praise God that he did not die in a snuffy bed of a trumpery cough, weakened by age, and saddened by the disappointments that would have attended his work had he lived."

Beckett was born in the determined Anglo-Irish Dublin suburb of Foxrock. He was Irish to his core. In fact, when a foreign journalist who was interviewing him asked, "Mister Beckett, you are British?" he swiftly replied, *"Au contraire!"* After fighting in the French resistance for four years during World War II, he went home to Ireland, joined the Irish Red Cross, and swiftly returned to France. Upon hearing the news of winning the Nobel he lamented, "Alas no Irish [whiskey] here—only Vat 69, or still lousier Donats."

5

THE IRISH FAMINE: FACT OR FICTION?

In New York City's Alphabet City, on the eastern edge of Tompkins Square Park, sits St. Brigid's Roman Catholic Church—famously known as the "Famine Church." It was built in 1848 by Irish immigrants who had just escaped the worst year of the Great Hunger, Black '47. Over its more than century-and-a-half history, the neighborhood has changed many times and there aren't many Irish left. But through a generous anonymous gift, the parish still lives, a symbol of the survival power—and perhaps stubbornness—of the impoverished Irish who built it.

Estimates vary but it is believed that out of a total Irish population of eight million in 1840, one million starved to death and 1.5 million emigrated. (Some scenarios have the population of the island being halved to four million during this decade.) Without the aid of gas chambers, ovens, or WMDs, the British somehow managed to remove millions of Irish men, women, and children from their native land.

It may seem strange, but the potato is not indigenous to Ireland. It is a South American plant and is believed to have been introduced to Ireland by Sir Walter Raleigh in the late sixteenth century. But to the native Irish, the potato became much more than a vegetable; it became their staple. It has been estimated that the average Irishman in mid-nineteenth century Ireland ate perhaps as many as fourteen pounds of potatoes *a day*. Remove the staple and the impoverished aborigines—who owned no land or property and survived at the whim of absentee landlords—faced starvation. The blight—*Phytophthora infestans*—started in America in 1843 and by 1845 it had arrived in Ireland.

The victims' deaths did not go unnoticed. Frederick Douglass, the African-American abolitionist, noted seeing families with nothing but "a board on a box for a table, rags on straw for a bed, and a picture of the crucifixion on the wall." John Mitchel, the Young Irelander, recorded in his *Jail Journal:* "Families, when all was eaten and no hope left, took their last look at the sun, built up their cottage doors that none might see them die nor hear their groans, and were found weeks afterwards, skeletons on their own hearth."

The question 160 years later is a confrontational one—was there ever really a famine in Ireland? Yes, there was blight on the potato, but at the same time the country was producing and exporting enough grain and livestock to feed the impoverished masses. John Mitchel, one of the bewildering figures of Irish revolutionary history—freedom fighter in Ireland, bigot in America—nailed it mightily when he noted that "the Almighty, indeed, sent the potato blight, but the English created the famine." Mitchel also opined that "if Yorkshire and Lancashire had sustained a like calamity in England, there is no doubt such measures as these would have been taken, promptly and liberally." For his outspokenness, Mitchel was convicted and deported.

Britain's reaction to the famine was a disaster. Prime Minister Sir Robert Peel purchased £100,000 worth of maize and corn from the United States, but it was nearly inedible and became known in Ireland as "Peel's brimstone." Soon Peel's government fell and he was replaced as prime minister by Lord John Russell. Russell introduced public works programs that were administered by Charles Trevelyan.

The British made a great show of their famine "relief." Queen Victoria even contributed £2,000 to it, but she is still remembered in Ireland as the "Famine Queen." The man in charge of famine relief, Trevelyan, seemed to relish in the suffering of the Irish who, in theory, he was supposed to be helping: "The judgment of God sent the calamity to teach the Irish a lesson, that calamity must not be too much mitigated. . . . The real evil with which we have to contend is not the physical evil of the Famine, but the moral evil of the selfish, perverse, and turbulent character of the people." He went on to describe the famine as "a direct stroke of an all-wise and all-merciful Providence," one which laid bare, "the deep and inveterate root of social evil." The famine, he declared, was "the sharp but effectual remedy by which the cure is likely to be effected. . . . God grant that the generation to which this great opportunity has been offered may rightly perform its part . . ." For confronting this "social evil," Trevelyan received a knighthood.

The exploitation of profit over people was also poignantly noted by Lady Jane Wilde—mother of Oscar Wilde—who wrote under the pseudonym "Speranza." Speranza was active in the Young Irelander movement and a friend of both John Mitchel and Thomas Davis, who wrote "A Nation Once Again." In her devastating poem "The Famine Year," she wrote:

> Weary man, what reap ye?—"Golden corn for the stranger."
> What sow ye?—"Human corpses that wait for the avenger."
> Fainting forms, hunger-stricken, what see ye in the offing?
> "Stately ships to bear our food away amid the stranger's scoffing."
> There's a proud array of soldiers—what do they round your door?
> "They guard our master's granaries from the thin hands of the poor."

She went on to write:

> Accursed are we in our own land, yet toil we still and toil;
> But the stranger reaps our harvest—the alien owns our soil.
> O Christ! how have we sinned, that on our native plains
> We perish homeless, naked, starved, with branded brow like Cain's?

And, at the end of the poem, Lady Wilde levels a warning for the British:

> But our whitening bones against ye will rise as witnesses,
> From the cabins and the ditches in their charred, uncoffined masses,
> For the Angel of the Trumpet will know them as he passes.
> A ghastly spectral army, before great God we'll stand,
> And arraign ye as our murderers, O spoilers of our land!"

In the worst year of the famine, Black 1847, some landlords tried to clear their land of the starving tenant farmers by shipping them off to North America. One such man was Major Denis Mahon, an absentee landlord from Stokestown in County Roscommon. Mahon shipped off a thousand souls to Québec aboard the infamous "Coffin Ships." It's been estimated that from one third to one half of these human beings died en route. But there would be repercussions for Mahon. He was gunned down by James Commins and Patrick Hasty in retribution. A troubled Queen Victoria noted in her diary: "A shocking murder has again taken placed in Ireland . . . Major Mahon, who had entirely devoted himself to being of use to the distressed Irish, was shot when driving home in his carriage. Really they are a terrible people, & there is no civilized country anywhere, which is in such a dreadful state, & where such crimes are perpetrated! It is a constant source of anxiety & annoyance." Yes, Victoria was right. The Irish are annoying—especially when starving.

Great Famine Memorial in Dublin

This was also the period of time when Protestant proselytizers tried to convert the starving Roman Catholics by offering them soup in return for the rejection of their religion. Those who did this were known as "taking the soup," and today, that phrase is still a terrible personal indictment to the Irish worldwide. (It should be noted that not all Protestant charities participated in this ghastly experiment and the Quakers are still remembered fondly in Ireland for their charity work during the famine.)

Today there are memorials to the victims of the famine in Ireland, England, the United States, Canada, and Australia. There is also Ireland's Great Hunger Institute at Quinnipiac University in Connecticut, under the directorship of Professor Christine Kinealy. And although the killers of Denis Mahon, Commins and Hasty, were executed, they may have had the last deadly laugh — the Irish National Famine Museum is located on the erstwhile estate of one Major Denis Mahon in Stokestown. (The museum is twinned with the Grosse Ile and the Irish National Historic Site in Grosse Ille, Quebec, Canada, the destination of Mahon's hired coffin ships.) The Irish National Famine Museum was opened in 1994 by Irish President Mary Robinson, who declared, "More than anything else, this Famine Museum shows us that history is not about power or triumph nearly so often as it is about suffering and vulnerability." It was something that another head of state, Queen Victoria, failed to realize.

In 1997 British Prime Minister Tony Blair said: "Those who governed in London at the time failed their people through standing by while a crop failure turned into a massive human tragedy. . . . That one million people died in what was then part of the richest and most powerful nation in the world is something that still causes pain as we reflect on it today."

6

CAN'T TELL THE REBELS
WITHOUT A SCORECARD

I n Ireland there will always be a throwaway reference to some (failed) moment in Irish history: "Sure Pearse and the lads didn't have a chance in the GPO, did they?"

You can admit your ignorance, nod your head with false sagacity, or know that "Pearse and the lads" in question were involved in the Easter Rising of 1916, where they were brutally crushed by the British forces.

So here are some historical figures and moments that every Irishman or would-be Irishman or woman should have in their rebel vocabulary:

The Patriots

Theobald Wolfe Tone, Lord Edward FitzGerald, Robert Emmet—this group of "modern" Irish revolutionaries were from the landed Protestant gentry and were members of the United Irishmen who fought the British with only pikes in the Uprising of 1798. They were annihilated by British infantry at the Battle of Vinegar Hill in Wexford, a moment in Irish history eerily brought to life by Nobel laureate Seamus Heaney. In his haunting poem "Requiem for the Croppies" he recalls how the rebels of 1798—the "croppies" because of their short, cropped hair—moved swiftly in rebellion:

> *The pockets of our greatcoats full of barley . . .*
> *No kitchens on the run, no striking camp . . .*
> *We moved quick and sudden in our own country . . .*

In defeat they were forgotten until their graves were marked:

> *And in August . . . the barley grew up out of our grave.*

The sacrifice of the United Irishmen was to inspire Irish patriots for nearly two hundred years.

Pádraig Pearse—the "President" of the Irish Republic, the existence of which he declared on the steps of the General Post Office (GPO) on Easter Monday, 1916. Under his command the occupying rebels held out for

Pádraig Pearse

nearly a week before surrendering. He was executed on May 3, 1916, by firing squad at Kilmainham Gaol.

James Connolly—Irish socialist labor leader and founder and commandant general of the Irish Citizen Army who was severely wounded in the leg at the GPO. His injuries were so severe that the British shot him in a chair at Kilmainham on May 12, 1916.

Thomas Clarke—the cagey old Fenian and the real force behind the Easter Rising. His nurturing of such young rebels as Seán Mac Diarmada, Joseph Mary Plunkett, and Pearse would change the course of Irish history. Naturalized in Brooklyn while in exile, he was the only American citizen to be executed by the British as a result of the skirmish, on May 3, 1916.

The Countess Markievicz—cocommander of St. Stephen's Green in 1916 and the first woman to ever hold a cabinet ministry. Read more about Markievicz in Chapter 7, "Ferocious Fenian Women."

Éamon de Valera—the senior commandant of the Easter Rising who was not executed because of his natural born American citizenship. He would be for the next fifty years either *Taoiseach* (prime minister) or president of the Republic of Ireland. He died in 1973 at the age of ninety-two.

Michael Collins—the legendary IRA leader and the father of the modern Irish state. During de Valera's absence in America during the War of Independence he systematically created an intelligence network that targeted British agents and spies. On the morning of November 21, 1920, his personal assassination squad eliminated most of the British secret service in Dublin. Just over twelve months later he signed the Treaty that created what is today the Republic of Ireland. He died in an ambush on August 22, 1922, at the age of thirty-one.

Sir Roger Casement—the last of the sixteen rebels executed for their participation in the Easter Rising. Casement's job during the Rising was to land rifles in County Kerry, which turned into an outright disaster. Captured by the British, he was brought to London to stand trial. During the trial, his notorious "Black Diaries" were leaked by the British goverment to suppress calls for his exoneration by such notables as George Bernard Shaw and Sir Arthur Conan Doyle. The diaries—still controversial to this day—allegedly revealed Casement's homosexual romps on two continents. He was hanged by the British on August 3, 1916, in Pentonville Prison in London. W.B. Yeats wrote a poem about him with the haunting refrain: *"The ghost of Roger Casement/Is beating on the door."*

Kevin Barry—an eighteen-year-old medical student and IRA volunteer, he was captured in northside Dublin in an ambush that went awry in October 1920. Despite cries for mercy, he was hanged in Mountjoy Prison on November 1, 1920—All Saints Day. One of Ireland's most popular rebel songs was written in his honor:

Another martyr for old Ireland,
Another murder for the crown,
Whose brutal laws may kill the Irish,
But can't keep their spirit down.
Lads like Barry are no cowards.
From the foe they will not fly.
Lads like Barry will free Ireland,
For her sake they'll live and die.

The 1916 Executions

The frenzy to execute the leaders of the Easter Rising began on May 3 and continued until May 12.

"I am going to ensure," said General Sir John Grenfell Maxwell, general officer commanding-in-chief of the British forces in Ireland, "that there will be no treason whispered for 100 years." Ignorantly, he began the process that would drive Britain out of most of Ireland for the first time in 700 years.

W.B. Yeats, in his poem, "Easter 1916," remembered the sacrifice of those who rose up and were executed for their efforts:

I write it out in a verse—
MacDonagh and MacBride
And Connolly and Pearse
Now and in time to be,
Wherever green is worn,

Are changed, changed utterly:
A terrible beauty is born.

Besides the aforementioned Pearse, Clarke, Connolly, and Casement, the honor roll of martyrs executed by the British in May 1916 include:

Thomas MacDonagh—poet, author, and schoolteacher, he was the commandant in charge of Jacob's Biscuit Factory, another skirmish location. He was a close friend and associate of Pádraig Pearse and taught at Pearse's school, St. Enda's in Rathfarnham. He was married to Muriel Gifford, Grace Gifford's sister. Executed by firing squad, Kilmainham Gaol, May 3, 1916.

Joseph Mary Plunkett—one of the most mysterious leaders, he served as the movement's foreign minister, traveling to Germany trying to drum up support for the coming insurrection. At the time of the Rising he was dying of tuberculosis of the neck glands. Michael Collins was his personal bodyguard and aide-de-camp. Hours before his execution he married his fiancée, Grace Gifford, in the Catholic chapel at Kilmainham. Immediately after the wedding he was taken out and shot on the morning of May 4, 1916. (See more on Grace Gifford Plunkett in Chapter 7, "Ferocious Fenian Women.")

Edward (Ned) Daly—commandant of the Four Courts. A member of the fiercely Fenian Daly family of Limerick. Brother of Kathleen Clarke and brother-in-law of Tom Clarke. Executed at Kilmainham, May 4, 1916.

Michael O'Hanrahan—vice commandant to Thomas McDonagh at Jacob's Biscuit Factory. Executed at Kilmainham on May 4, 1916.

William (Willie) Pearse—the younger brother of Pádraig Pearse, which was the main reason he was executed. Although he held the rank of captain in the Irish Volunteers, he was not part of the senior leadership. He was a talented sculptor and his work can be viewed at the Pearse Museum in Rathfarnham, St. Andrew's Church, Westland Row, and St. Stephen's Green. Executed at Kilmainham on May 4, 1916.

John (Seán) MacBride—was on his way to his brother's wedding reception when he ran into the revolution and decided to take part, fighting at Jacob's. Husband of Maud Gonne and father of Seán MacBride, who would go on to win the Nobel Peace Prize in 1974. His hatred of the British led him to go as far as South Africa to fight against them in the Boer War. Although he was a romantic rival for Maud Gonne with William Butler Yeats, Yeats remembered him in "Easter 1916" as *"A drunken, vainglorious lout . . . Yet I number him in the song."* Executed at Kilmainham on May 5, 1916.

Seán Mac Diarmada

Éamonn Ceannt—cofounder of the Irish Volunteers, he commanded the South Dublin Union during the Rising. Executed at Kilmainham on May 8, 1916.

Conn Colbert—commanded the rebels at the Marrowbone Lane Distillery, not far from the Guinness Brewery. Executed at Kilmainham on May 8, 1916.

Seán Heuston—a railroad worker, Heuston commanded the Mendicity Institution on the River Liffey, holding off the British for several days. The nearby Heuston Railroad Station, where Seán worked, is named in his honor. Executed at Kilmainham on May 8, 1916.

Michael Mallin—chief of staff of Connolly's Irish Citizen Army, he commanded, along with the Countess Markievicz, St. Stephen's Green and the College of Surgeons during the Rising. Executed at Kilmainham on May 8, 1916.

Thomas Kent—along with Sir Roger Casement, he was the only rebel not to be executed at Kilmainham. Executed at Cork Detention Barracks on May 9, 1916.

Seán Mac Diarmada (John McDermott)—next to Tom Clarke, he may have been the most influential man behind the Rising. He was a master organizer and people were drawn to the movement because of his charismatic character. A former Belfast barman, he was stricken with polio in 1912. Executed at Kilmainham on May 12, 1916.

Yeats remembered the executed rebels in his poem, "Sixteen Dead Men":

O but we talked at large before
The sixteen men were shot,
But who can talk of give and take,
What should be and what not
While those dead men are loitering there
To stir the boiling pot?

The Events

The War of Independence—the name given to the struggle for Irish independence during the years 1916–1921.

GPO—the General Post Office, O'Connell Street, Dublin, where the Easter Rising began on Monday, April 24, 1916. It is the most important building in Irish history and is still functioning as an active post office.

Kilmainham Gaol—this eighteenth century prison fortress is located on the south side of Dublin. In the weeks following the Easter Rising fourteen leaders were executed here by firing squad. A riveting, albeit disturbing, tour of the prison and the breaker's yard where the rebels were executed should be on every tourist's must-do list.

Glasnevin Cemetery—located on the northside of Dublin minutes from the City Centre, this is the final resting place of many a famous Irishman from Parnell to Brendan Behan. It is, however, the place where most of Ireland's revolutionaries are planted, including Michael Collins and Éamon de Valera. You can visit the grave of Sir Roger Casement and Kevin Barry and visit the appropriately named Republican Plot where the likes of Cathal Brugha, Harry Boland, John Devoy, and Jeremiah O'Donovan Rossa are interred. It was at Rossa's grave in August 1915 that Pádraig Pearse made his famous speech proclaiming, "The fools, the fools, the fools, they have left us our Fenian dead."

IRB versus IRA—everyone knows what the Irish Republican Army (IRA) is, but many are confused about what the Irish Republican Brotherhood (IRB) was. The IRB was formed in 1859 in New York City by John O'Mahony and its members were known as "Fenians" because they were followers of the ancient Celtic warrior, Finn. It was a highly secretive organization, dedicated to freeing Ireland from British rule by force. Many of its members participated in the Rising of '67 and spent time in prison. (They also invaded Canada twice from the United States.) In the 1880s, another branch called "The Invincibles" terrorized the British both in Ireland and England. Almost all the hierarchy of the Easter Rising were members of the IRB, and its last head was Michael Collins. It effectively died with Collins in 1922.

Bloody Sunday—there are three "Bloody Sundays" in modern Irish history. The first one occurred in 1913 when police charged striking workers in O'Connell Street; the second was in 1920 when Michael Collins's agents assassinated fourteen agents of the British Secret Service in Dublin and the British retaliated by firing into the crowd at a football match in Croke Park, killing another fourteen; the last occurred in 1972 when the British army, unprovoked, murdered fourteen civil rights protesters in Derry.

The Treaty—the name given to the piece of paper Michael Collins signed on December 6, 1921, creating the Irish Free State, which eventually evolved into the Republic of Ireland in 1949.

Civil War—the conflict between pro- (Collins) and anti- (de Valera) Treaty forces in 1922–23. It left scars that have only disappeared in the last few years.

Béal na mBláth—the area of County Cork where Michael Collins was gunned down. In Irish it means "the mouth or the gap of the flowers." Brendan Behan's mother, Kathleen, always called Collins her "laughing boy" and Behan wrote his most famous poem, "The Laughing Boy," about Collins's death.

> *It was on an August morning, all in the morning hours,*
> *I went to take the warming air all in the month of flowers,*
> *And there I saw a maiden and heard her mournful cry,*
> *Oh, what will mend my broken heart, I've lost my Laughing Boy.*

The Twelve Apostles—the nickname given to Michael Collins's personal assassination squad, famous for shooting most of the British secret service in Dublin on Bloody Sunday, 1920. Members included:

Vinny Byrne, who started out in Jacob's Biscuit Factory in 1916 at the age of fifteen and by 1922 was a commandant-colonel in the Free State Army. Vinny was an extremely active member of the Squad and responsible for the slayings on Bloody Sunday at 38 Upper Mount Street. In old age he described for a joint BBC/RTE history of Ireland what happened that day: "I put the two of them up against the wall. May the Lord have mercy on your souls. I plugged the two of them."

Mick O'Donnell and **Paddy Daly** were two of the leaders of the Squad. Daly, from Parnell Street, went on to be a general under Michael Collins during the Irish Civil War.

Charlie Dalton wrote a wonderful reminiscence of the War of Independence called *With the Dublin Brigade,* in which he describes the utter terror he experienced on Bloody Sunday.

The scope of the Bloody Sunday operation was so huge that the members of the Squad could not handle it by themselves. Therefore, members of the Dublin brigade were brought in to supplement them. One of these members was **Seán Lemass**, who shot British agents in Baggot Street. Lemass went on to serve in de Valera's cabinet and was responsible for the establishment of both Aer Lingus and Ardmore Studios before he became *Taoiseach* in 1959. He was the first *Taoiseach* to travel to the North, trying to find common ground between the two governments of Ireland. He has, perhaps, the greatest quote about his short time in the Squad: "Firing squads don't have reunions!"

7

FEROCIOUS FENIAN WOMEN

I f you thought the bold Fenian men were tough, you'll be shocked to see that they had nothing on the ferocious Fenian women.

The backbone of the Irish Volunteers (and later the IRA) were fierce rebel women, who were often members of the **Cumann na mBan**, the IRA's women auxiliary (translated as the "Irishwomen's Council"). The *Cumann* was established at Wynn's Hotel in Lower Abbey Street in 1914. During the Rising they supported the insurgents as couriers, nurses, cooks, etc. One of their members, Margaretta Keough, was killed during the battle at the South Dublin Union.

During the War of Independence they were often the backbone of the movement since so many IRA men were imprisoned or "on the run." They helped run the *Dáil* courts, served in the propaganda ministry, and hid wanted men and arms. They, almost to a woman, went against the Treaty Michael Collins brought back from London, voting 419-63 against it.

The Countess Markievicz

Constance Gore-Booth was born in London of Anglo-Irish stock in 1868. After her marriage to a Polish count she was thereafter known as the Countess Markievicz. She was cocommander of St. Stephen's Green in 1916 and the only reason she was not executed was because she was a woman. ("I do wish your lot had the decency to shoot me," she told the British at her court-martial.) A leader of the *Cumann* when she was not in prison, she was elected to the *Dáil* in the general election of 1918 and became the first woman in the world to hold a cabinet position (Minister for Labor) in the first *Dáil*. Uncompromising in her Republican beliefs to the end, she died in 1927. Although Yeats and the Countess were on

Countess Markievicz

opposite sides after the Treaty, he remembered her and her sister in "In Memory of Eva Gore-Booth and Con Markievicz":
The older is condemned to death,
Pardoned, drags out lonely years
Conspiring among the ignorant.

Maud Gonne

Maud was born in England in 1866. Educated in France, she first went to Ireland in 1882 when her father, a British army officer, was posted in Dublin. There, in the time of the Fenians known as the "Invincibles," she caught the revolutionary bug, which would remain with her for the rest of her life. She is credited with nicknaming Queen Victoria "the Famine Queen." Her personal life was as tumultuous as her political life. While in Ireland, William Butler Yeats fell in love with her and would obsess and lust after her for the rest of his life. (She rejected him, spouting the great axiom: "Poets should never marry.")

Maud Gonne

In 1900 she founded *Inghinidhe na hÉireann* (translated as "Daughters of Ireland), the forerunner to the *Cumann na mBan*. Like Markievicz, she would be a convert to Catholicism and in 1904 she would marry the radical Irish nationalist, John MacBride. The next year their son, future Nobel Peace Prize laureate, Seán, would be born. She soon acrimoniously divorced MacBride and raised her child in Paris. After MacBride's execution in 1916 she returned to Dublin.

During the War for Independence she was imprisoned in England with Markievicz and Kathleen Clarke. She, of course, opposed the Treaty. (Ironically, her son Seán MacBride, as Minister for External Affairs in the coalition government of 1949, was instrumental in declaring the Republic of Ireland.) She spent much of her life doing good works for the poor and those shunned by society. She died in Belfast in 1953 and is buried in Glasnevin Cemetery in Dublin.

Kathleen Clarke

A member of the radical nationalist Daly family of Limerick, Kathleen naturally married the tough old Fenian Tom Clarke. After living for a period in New York, they returned to Dublin in 1907 as Clarke started the buildup which would result in the Easter Rising of 1916. In the Rising, she suffered a triple loss: her husband was executed; her brother Ned, commandant in charge of the Four Courts, was executed; and she suffered a miscarriage shortly thereafter. Her book, *Revolutionary Woman*, tells many secrets about the Rising and what her husband thought of Eoin MacNeill, who countermanded the orders which would have had the Rising begin on Easter Sunday. She gave Michael Collins his first job in 1917, which would lead to Collins controlling the revolution when de Valera abdicated to go to America for twenty months in 1919. During the War of Independence, she was imprisoned in England. She became the first female Lord Mayor of Dublin in 1939. One of her first official acts was to remove a portrait of Queen Victoria from the Mansion House. No rubber stamp for de Valera, she opposed his Constitution of 1937 because she believed it was antifeminist. She helped found the Irish Red Cross. She died in 1972, an amazing fifty-six years after her husband's execution.

Charlotte Despard

Charlotte was one of the most unlikely—and colorful—Irish rebels in that she was the sister of the British Viceroy, Lord French, one of the most hated symbols of the British occupation of Ireland. She was born in England in 1844, and by the turn of the century she was an advocate for the London poor, an opponent of the Boer War, and an active suffragette. During the War of Independence, she joined up with Maud Gonne to found the Women's Prisoners' Defence League, and as a member of the *Cumann na mBan* she was anti-Treaty. In later life she became infatuated with the Communist Party. She died 1939 and joined her friend Maud Gonne in Glasnevin's Republican Plot.

Estella Solomons

Although probably best remembered for her artistic endeavors, Solomons was also a *Cumann na mBan* member. In fact, she may have been the only Jewish member of that organization. Trained at the Dublin Metropolitan School of Art, also in Paris and London, she became part of the Irish impressionist school. Her portraits include such famous Irishmen as Arthur Griffith, Jack Yeats, James Stephens, Padraic Colum, and Count Plunkett. She joined the *Cumann na mBan* in 1917 and was an active member of the struggle for independence. Among her feats was stealing her British brother-in-law's army uniform for the IRA and hiding and distributing weapons and ammunition. Like most members of the *Cumann,* she voted against the Treaty. She later married Seamus O'Sullivan, editor of *The Dublin Magazine,* one of the eponymous Irish literary magazines.

Dorothy Macardle

A member of *Cumann na mBan* since 1917, she was an ardent Republican and a founding member of the *Fianna Fáil* party. She went against the Treaty and was imprisoned in both Kilmainham and Mountjoy Gaols. She is, however, best remembered as a writer, and her novel, *Uneasy Freehold*, was made into one of the all-time great ghost movies, *The Uninvited* (1944), starring Ray Milland and Gail Russell.

Grace Gifford's Secret

Perhaps the most romantic story in all of Fenian lore is the candlelight marriage of **Grace Gifford** and Joseph Mary Plunkett in the Catholic chapel of Kilmainham Gaol hours before Joe was executed by firing squad on May 4, 1916. It is a major part of the Kilmainham tour, and Frank and Seán O'Meara even wrote a haunting song about it from the perspective of Joe Plunkett called, simply, "Grace." It is popularly performed by many groups in Ireland.

Grace Gifford

Joe Plunkett was a mysterious figure in his own right, but the aura surrounding Grace is also shrouded in mystery. She is often portrayed as a solitary artist, staunch Republican, largely ignored by the Plunkett family, a neglected figure who died by herself in her South Richmond Street flat in Dublin in 1955. But Geraldine Plunkett Dillon, Joe's sister, paints a very different, unromantic picture of Grace in her autobiography, *All in the Blood,* and also reveals Grace's biggest secret.

". . . [W]hile she was staying in Larkfield," Geraldine wrote, "she took every advantage of the position; she was destructive and a messer and I thought her silly and dangerous. . . . The family solicitor had told me to let Larkfield, so I had moved Grace to Fitzwilliam Street and when she left there the place was an awful mess. She took things and sold them or gave them away. Money or possessions meant nothing to her except to play with for a little while and then give away to the first person who asked."

Grace was always in need of money although she received government pensions, including one when Éamon de Valera became president in 1932. Geraldine recalls that "Grace started ringing up Pa [Count Plunkett] saying she must have £50 or she would kill herself. Even Pa got tired of this after giving her the money the first few times."

Like Kathleen Clarke, she suffered multiple personal losses in the 1916 Rising—she lost her husband and her brother-in-law, Thomas MacDonagh, who was married to her sister Muriel. She also suffered a miscarriage.

Geraldine Plunkett answers one of the great questions of the Easter Rising—was Grace Gifford pregnant when she married Joe Plunkett? This may seem an irrelevant question today, but remember the Catholic Dublin of 1916—pious and unrelenting. Grace had converted to Catholicism early in April 1916 and her desperate marriage just before Joe's execution had set those pious Dublin tongues awaggin'.

Geraldine leaves no doubt about Grace's situation with this first-hand account: "I went out to Larkfield to see Grace and was told that she was upstairs in bed. When I went into her bedroom I saw a large white chamberpot full of blood and foetus. She said nothing and I said nothing."

Mystery solved.

8

HOW MICHAEL COLLINS HELPED SAVE WINSTON CHURCHILL'S CAREER

Today Winston Churchill is thought of as an icon of democracy—especially by those who know nothing of Churchill's personal history.

World War I was not very kind to Churchill. In May of 1915 the *Lusitania* was sunk under his watch as First Lord of the Admiralty. Earlier that same year he came up with his great Ottoman Empire adventure in Gallipoli where he found that "Johnny Turkey" was more than a match for the British and their Australian and French allies. Churchill's campaign in the Dardanelles was an utter disaster that nearly collapsed Prime Minister Asquith's government and would lead Churchill himself out of office and to the trenches in France.

By 1919 Churchill's career was in dry dock, although he was back in Prime Minister David Lloyd George's government as secretary of state for war. His problem this time was not the Turks, but another Dardanelles problem. In Dublin, under the direction of Michael Collins, guerrilla warfare was turning deadly.

In South Dublin there is one long thoroughfare—the streets named Camden, Wexford, Aungier, and Georges—one has to pass if you're coming from the Portobello Barracks in Rathmines and heading to Dublin Castle. Every day, convoys of British troops passed this way. The second battalion of the IRA took umbrage and started tossing hand grenades into the lorries. The British put chicken wire over their trucks so the grenades would bounce back to their originators but a fishhook solved that problem and the carnage continued. The British found that the only way to gain safe passage was to seat a well-known citizen as a hostage. The locals began to call this long thoroughfare the "Dardanelles." The children soon retrieved a song from the Great War—some say written by Seán O'Casey—called "The Grand Ould Dame Britannia":

> *"What's the news the newsboy yells?*
> *What's the news the paper tells?*
> *A British retreat from the Dardanelles?"*
> *Says the Grand Old Dame Britannia*

By late 1919, Michael Collins, as director of intelligence of the IRA, identified the main reason why Irish rebels had *always* failed— the superior British intelligence agencies, fueled by informers. He decided to attack the problem at its origin—the "G" Division of the Dublin Metropolitan Police. This was the section that dealt with "political" dissidents, i.e., the IRA. Collins warned, then threatened, these intelligence coppers to get out; if they didn't, he would permanently remove them. To do this he established his personal assassination squad, which could only shoot on the orders of Collins and his two deputies, Richard Mulcahy, IRA chief of staff, and Dick McKee, commandant of the Dublin IRA brigades. Soon this Squad was calling themselves the "Twelve Apostles."

In early 1920 Churchill decided that the Royal Irish Constabulary (RIC), the police force of the country, needed reinforcements. Churchill introduced the Auxiliaries, often known as the "Auxies." Later a second group of temporary constables for the RIC was introduced. They were soon nicknamed the "Black and Tans" because of their rag-tag uniforms. Together, the Auxies and the Tans would terrorize the Irish people for nearly two years.

Collins continued the systematic removal of eager G-men, and by the spring of 1920 he had a bigger problem on his hands that would soon bring him to the personal attention of Secretary Churchill.

Collins was the first minister for finance for the new country. Under this portfolio he was charged with raising a national loan to feed the financial needs of the infant nation. Money was raised and hidden in banks in America and Ireland. The British had prohibited the Loan and were now in search of the money. They sent a man by the name of Alan Bell to Dublin to find the dough. Bell, a man in his sixties, had been playing with Fenians from the time of Parnell's Land League. After he confiscated £18,000 in Loan funds, Collins decided he had to go. On the morning of March 26, 1920, he was pulled off a tram on his way to work at Dublin Castle by the Squad and shot dead. Mission Accomplished—no more bank examiners were volunteering for Dublin duty. This blatant act immediately caught the eye of Churchill and shocked him. "Really getting very serious," he wrote to his wife Clementine. "What a diabolical streak [the Irish] have in their character! I expect it is that treacherous, assassinating, conspiring trait which has done them in in bygone ages of history and prevented them from being a great responsible nation with stability and prosperity. It is shocking that we have not been able to bring the murderers to justice."

Churchill soon put a £5,000—sometimes embellished to £10,000—reward on the man responsible for Bell's death. The man responsible for Bell's death was Michael Collins—and a legend was born.

On the morning of November 21, 1920, Collins's Squad struck the ultimate blow when they assassinated fourteen British secret service agents on "Bloody Sunday." For all intents and purposes the war was over, but murder would rule on both sides until July 1921, when a Truce, with the help of King George V, was called. By October, against his own wishes, Collins found himself leading the Irish delegation—along with Arthur Griffith—at the treaty talks in 10 Downing Street because de Valera refused to go himself, although he was the president of the Irish parliament. Churchill sat opposite Collins and stared. But Churchill admired courage and over the weeks came to admire the Dublin Pimpernel, a man of action, just the kind of man Churchill saw in himself.

Churchill's first instinct was always to be bellicose. Now his wife, Clementine, tried to temper the instinct that had always gotten Churchill into trouble. "Do my darling," she wrote him, "use your influence now for some sort of moderation or at any rate justice in Ireland. Put yourself in the place of the Irish. If you were their leader you would not be cowed by severity & certainly not by reprisals which fall like the rain from Heaven upon the Just & upon the Unjust. . . . It always makes me unhappy and disappointed when I see you inclined to take for granted that the rough iron-fisted 'hunnish' way will prevail."

Apparently, Clementine's "Hun" reference had an effect. One night in late November with the negotiations stalemated, Churchill invited Collins, Arthur Griffith, Lloyd George, and Lord Birkinhead back to his townhouse for drinks. Griffith went upstairs with the prime minister and Collins while Churchill and Birkinhead remained on the ground floor.

And they started to drink. Cognac. Collins, always with a sweet tooth, wanted his spiked with curaçao. And they drank more.

Michael Collins

Soon the conversation turned ugly. The question of the loyalty oath to the king piqued Collins's inner-Fenian. He suddenly turned on Churchill in such a threatening manner that Churchill, years later, wrote that "He was in his most difficult mood, full of reproaches and defiances, and it was very easy for everyone to lose his temper."

"You put a £5,000 pound bounty on my head," Collins bellowed at Churchill. Birkinhead was sure blows were about to be struck. But Churchill quietly took Collins by the hand and brought him to the other end of the room. There, on the wall, was a wanted poster from the Boer War for one Winston Spencer Churchill—for £25!

"At least I put a good amount on your head!" said Churchill.

Collins laughed and the tension was broken. From that day onward Churchill was part of the solution in Ireland, not the problem. Churchill, now secretary of state for the colonies, worked hand-in-hand with Collins and Griffith to birth the new Irish Free State. After the deaths of Griffith and Collins, he continued to help the new state. It was a sign of growth and maturity on Churchill's part that he could go from warmonger to peacemaker.

Upon Collins's death Churchill wrote: "He was an Irish patriot, true and fearless. . . . When in future times the Irish Free State is not only prosperous and happy, but an active and annealing force . . . regard will be paid by widening circles to his life and to his death. . . . Successor to a sinister inheritance, reared among fierce conditions and moving through ferocious times, he supplied those qualities of action and personality without which the foundations of Irish nationhood would not have been reestablished." For the rest of his life, Churchill always referred to Collins as "General Collins"—high praise indeed.

After the firm establishment of the Irish Free State, Churchill would continue to hold office until the depression. Then, he found himself in the political wilderness. But, unlike Lloyd George, he would not find himself tripping to Berchtesgaden to prostrate himself before Adolf Hitler in admiration. Perhaps he had learned something from Michael Collins—never bend the knee to the tyrant.

9

MICHAEL COLLINS:
SEX AND THE SINGLE
REVOLUTIONARY

Michael Collins has been dead for over ninety years, but the world's fascination with him continues to grow. Collins, perhaps the most dynamic and innovative revolutionary of the twentieth century, has many admirers. The Israelis basically copied his revolutionary plans which banished the British from Ireland, and applied them to Palestine. He was admired by future Israeli Prime Minister Yitzhak Shamir, Mao Tse-tung, and even the young Nelson Mandela. Recently, there has been as much interest in his sex life as there ever was in his revolutionary tenets.

When he died at the age of thirty-one in 1922, he was engaged to Kitty Kiernan. But it was during the Treaty negotiations of October–December 1921 that the world's press focused on Collins, suggesting that he was not only a statesman but perhaps the Irish answer to Don Juan. For it was during this period when his path converged with several women, including Lady Hazel Lavery, American wife of the famous painter, Sir John Lavery, and Moya Llewelyn-Davies.

Collins used Lady Lavery as a diplomatic go-between because of her social connections within the British power structure. She often drove him around London for meetings and social functions. It was these events that set tongues a-waggin'. Were they intimate? Of course, no one knows for sure. But years later some of Collins's poetry was discovered, and in it there was his ode to Lady Lavery:

> Oh! Hazel, Hazel Lavery:
> What is your charm Oh! Say?
> Like subtle Scottish Mary

Lady Hazel Lavery

You take my heart away.
Not by your wit and beauty
Nor your delicate sad grace
Nor the golden eyes of wonder
In the flower that is your face.

I'll leave the Lady Lavery–Collins relationship up to the historians, but revolutionaries—particularly *Irish* revolutionaries—don't usually write poems describing their subject as having "wit and beauty" unless there is an underlying passion.

Collins's relationship with Moya Llewelyn-Davies is more complicated. Was she a lover, just a friend, or, as some have maintained, a stalker? Collins apparently knew her when he was living in London between 1906 and 1915. In fact, Vincent McDowell in *Michael Collins and the Brotherhood* claims that Llewelyn-Davies's son, Richard, born in 1912, was the biological child of Michael Collins. Richard, later in his life, used to brag about his paternity. Unfortunately, Richard Llewelyn Davies went to his grave without leaving us a DNA test.

With the possibility of Collins "entertaining" three women in the fall of 1921, it is surprising to hear that he probably went to the grave a virgin! This is the conclusion of University College Dublin professor of modern history Diarmaid Ferriter: "I've never seen any kind of proof that Collins was ever sexually active. I believe he died a virgin."

John A. Murphy, professor emeritus of history at University College Cork, took a similar approach. "Collins has sometimes been wrenched from his proper historical context and forced into contemporary relevance," Murphy said. "Thus, he is depicted as a very modern 'macho' man, cast in a late twentieth-century mold, especially in the area of sexual permissiveness. However, his alleged womanizing remains mere speculation and there is no evidence he succumbed to the blandishments of his groupies. He was exclusively devoted to his fiancée Kitty Kiernan. He was a practicing Catholic after the manner of his day, even if occasionally anticlerical in the Fenian tradition."

On the other hand, openly gay Irish Senator David Norris (see chapter 15, Gay Gaels, for more on Norris) now claims that Collins was gay! In his autobiography, *A Kick Against the Pricks*, Norris claims that one of Collins's grand-nephews spilled the beans to him: "I had a chat with him in the coffee bar and was greatly amused to hear that, according to him, he shared this [gay] trait with his great-uncle. I don't know if he was teasing or not but a subsequent event appeared to confirm it. An elderly man came in one night who had been visiting *Sinn Fein*'s headquarters three doors down. He had fought in the Civil War more than half a century before and claimed to have been one of Michael Collins's principal boyfriends." Norris went on to add that: "I mentioned this to a well-known popular historian of the period, who confirmed that this was generally known in certain republican circles."

On hearing Norris's claim, Ferriter (of the virgin school) suggested that it was "wishful thinking on David's part."

Of course, one wonders if Michael Collins had been a failure as a revolutionary if people would have cared one way or another about his sexuality. As President Kennedy, another man with an eye for the ladies, once remarked, "Victory has a thousand fathers, but defeat is an orphan."

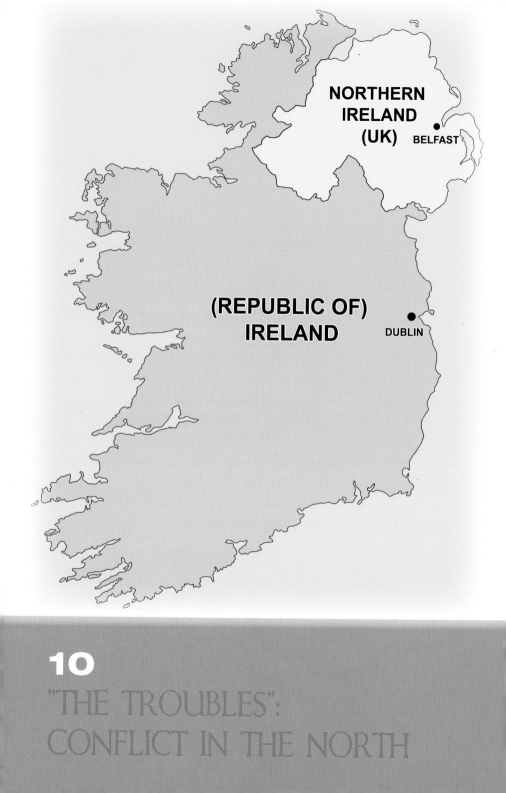

NORTHERN
IRELAND
(UK)   BELFAST

(REPUBLIC OF)
IRELAND   DUBLIN

10
"THE TROUBLES":
CONFLICT IN THE NORTH

The Reverend Martin Luther King Jr.'s civil rights campaign in the United States in the 1960s had a tremendous effect on the Catholics of Northern Ireland. They came to identify with the blacks of the Old Confederacy who lived under a very American apartheid since President Lincoln's emancipation a hundred years before. They decided, like Dr. King, to organize and non-violently protest their second-class citizenship in Northern Ireland, considered by many Catholics to be a bastard annex of the United Kingdom.

Peacefully, the Catholics sought better housing, better jobs, the end to gerrymandering—which was rendering their votes powerless—and reform of the Royal Ulster Constabulary (RUC), which was little more than a bigoted arm of the Northern Ireland government. Catholic demands were met with sectarian murder and, like in Alabama, their marches were banned by the local authorities. The Catholics, it seemed, had gotten the attention of their Protestant masters.

Catholic protesters were harassed and beaten by local Protestant paramilitary forces. But more disturbingly, they were pounced on by members of the RUC, many of whom were off duty at the time. It was becoming obvious to the Catholics that they could not count on the police to protect them. By August 1969, the situation had degenerated to such a degree that the Irish *Taoiseach*, Jack Lynch, declared that the Irish government "can no longer stand by and see innocent people injured and perhaps worse." Soon thereafter the British sent in the first troops to keep the peace—and the IRA was soon back in business. In 1971, as the situation disintegrated, internment without trial was introduced by the British government.

Bobby Sands

The next several years brought seemingly ceaseless conflict, including Bloody Sunday in Derry and the collapse of the Stormont government. British Prime Minister Harold Wilson brought about the ineffective Sunningdale Agreement, which was disliked by both the militant Protestants and the IRA. The return to violence was swift, as if ingrained in both sides.

On May 5, 1981, Bobby Sands, MP and member of the Provisional IRA—following the 1920 example of Terence MacSwiney, the lord mayor of Cork—starved himself to death after sixty-six days on a hunger strike. That same day British Prime Minister Margaret Thatcher—proving she never heard the lament of George Santayana that "Those who cannot remember the past are condemned to repeat it"—said in the House of Commons: "Mr. Sands was a convicted criminal. He chose to take his own life. It was a choice that his organization [the IRA] did not allow to many of its victims."

Thatcher didn't know it at the time, but something powerful had just happened that would change the history of Northern Ireland. By 1985 the Anglo-Irish Agreement came into effect, giving the Republic an advisory role in the affairs of Northern Ireland.

It would take another thirteen years and many atrocities by both sides, but peace—largely through the efforts of American President Bill Clinton—would finally come to the peoples of Northern Ireland. Here are a few of the people and events that made peace possible.

The Players

John Hume—a founding member of the Social Democratic and Labour Party (SDLP), he was always a quiet, behind-the-scenes player in the development of the peace in Northern Ireland. In 1998 he won the Nobel Peace Prize (shared with Unionist David Trimble) for his work in the peace process.

Gerry Adams—head of *Sinn Féin*, the political arm of the Provisional IRA. Adams was imprisoned many times by the British for his political activities, although he maintains to this day that he was never a member of the IRA. In 1983 he was elected MP, but refused to take his seat at Westminster. The following year he was the victim of a Protestant assassination attempt, but he survived his wounds. He would play a pivotal part in the Good Friday Agreement of 1998. In 2010 he was elected TD to *Dáil Éireann*, representing Louth.

Martin McGuinness—former leader of the Provisional IRA in Derry. In 1973 he served six months time in the Republic for being apprehended with bomb-making materials. He claims he resigned from the IRA in 1974 and turned to politics, playing a prominent part in *Sinn Féin*. Since then he has been both an absentee MP to Westmin-

Gerry Adams

ster and the Northern Ireland Assembly in Stormont. He became *Sinn Féin*'s chief negotiator in the period leading up to the Good Friday Agreement. Presently he is deputy first minister of Northern Ireland. He ran unsuccessfully for president of the Irish Republic in 2011.

Bernadette Devlin McAliskey—for the period of 1969–74 she was an MP at Westminster and became the face of the Catholic minority in their Ulster struggle. Elected MP at the age of twenty-one, she was, and remains, the youngest woman ever elected to the British parliament. She's atypical of nationalist MPs from the North in that she took her seat at Westminster. She was present at both the Battle of the Bogside in 1969 and Bloody Sunday in 1972. In 1981 she was shot in front of her children at her home in County Tyrone and although wounded seven times, she survived. Since losing her seat in parliament in 1974, she has run for office on both sides of the border without success. She remains a think-outside-the-box socialist in the mode of James Connolly.

Rev. Ian Paisley—the face and the voice of the Protestant majority since the beginning of the Troubles. A fundamentalist minister, Paisley's views on social issues like dancing ("Line dancing . . . is an incitement to lust") and homosexuality ("Save Ulster from Sodomy") had more in common with the Catholic Church than he would have liked to admit. He had a history of provoking Catholics going back to the early 1950s over such things as flying the Irish tricolour and religious conversions. He opposed both the Sunning-dale Agreement and the Anglo-Irish Agreement of 1985. Initially opposed to the Good Friday Agreement, he subsequently became a minister in the power-sharing agreement and in 2007 became the first minister of Northern Ireland, working alongside his first deputy, former IRA gunman Martin McGuinness. His change in politics is often credited with helping to bring about the end of sectarian violence in Northern Ireland. He died on September 12, 2014.

David Trimble—elected leader of the Ulster Unionist Party in 1995, Trimble would be at the helm of the party just as seismic changes were about to happen to Northern Ireland politics. Trimble moved rapidly after assuming the leadership—meeting with the Irish *Taoiseach* in Dublin and then becoming the first Unionist leader to meet with *Sinn Féin* since the partition of the island in 1922. Although he had a chilly relationship with Gerry Adams he worked to achieve the Good Friday Agreement and in 1998 became the first minister of Northern Ireland. In October 1998 he shared the Nobel Peace Prize with John Hume for their effort in bringing peace to Northern Ireland. The Nobel Institute noted that Trimble "showed great political courage."

The Good Friday Agreement

Brokered by President Bill Clinton and birthed by former U.S. Senator George Mitchell, the Good Friday Agreement of 1998 finally found common cause and laid the groundwork for peace in Northern Ireland. It was ushered in by the likes of John Hume, Gerry Adams, Martin McGuinness, and David Trimble along with British Prime Minister Tony Blair and Irish *Taoiseach* Bertie Ahern. It was approved by the voters of both the Irish Republic and Northern Ireland.

Police Service of Northern Ireland

One of the important developments of the Good Friday Agreement was the restructuring of the Royal Ulster Constabulary (RUC) into the PSNI. Since the inception of the Northern Ireland state, Catholics had viewed the RUC (reshaped from the Royal Irish Constabulary after the establishment of Irish Free State in 1922) as a part of the power structure of the Northern Ireland government—i.e., put there to keep them in their place. With the reorganization of the PSNI, Catholics, as of 2011, make up almost 30 percent of the force.

Reconciliation

As part of the healing process, both the British Prime Minister, David Cameron, and the British head-of-state, Queen Elizabeth II, have addressed the events and the consequences of what has happened over the past 800 years in Ireland:

> *"What happened on Bloody Sunday was both unjustified and unjustifiable. It was wrong . . .You do not defend the British Army by defending the indefensible. . . . It is clear from the tribunal's authoritative conclusions that the events of Bloody Sunday were in no way justified. . . . I know that some people wonder whether, nearly forty years on from an event [if] a prime minister needs to issue an apology. . . . But what happened should never, ever have happened. The families of those who died should not have had to live with the pain and the hurt of that day and with a lifetime of loss. Some members of our armed forces acted wrongly. The government is ultimately responsible for the conduct of the armed forces and for that, on behalf of the government, indeed, on behalf of our country. I am deeply sorry."*
>
> —David Cameron, British Prime Minister, commenting on the Saville Inquiry of 2010 into the events of Bloody Sunday in Derry, January 30, 1972

> *"To all those who have suffered as a consequence of our troubled past I extend my sincere thoughts and deep sympathy. With the benefit of historical hindsight we can all see things which we would wish had been done differently or not at all."*
>
> —Queen Elizabeth II on her state visit to the Republic of Ireland, Dublin Castle, May 2011

11

THE IRISH DIASPORA:
TAKING A PART OF
IRELAND WITH YOU

The Random House College Dictionary defines the term "diaspora" as "the scattering of Jews to countries outside of Palestine after the Babylonian captivity." Merriam-Webster.com gives a more modern definition: "a group of people who live outside the area in which they had lived for a long time or in which their ancestors lived." That pretty much describes the Irish, especially since the time of the Great Famine of the 1840s when the population of the island was perhaps halved. But it cannot be denied that the Irish have always liked to travel. Check the history of almost any country and you'll find an Irishman somehow intimately involved in their history.

The history of Australia is populated with Irish names—many of whom were sent there for their part in some insurrection. It is estimated that 40,000 were shipped to Australia because of their participation in revolutionary acts between the risings of 1798 and 1867. (In fact, it was the great American Fenian, the daring John Devoy, who rescued many of the men of '67 by sending the American ship, the *Catalpa*, to their aid in 1875.) Familiar Irish-Australian names include the outlaw Ned Kelly, Thomas Keneally, author of *Schindler's Ark* (which would be adapted into *Schindler's List* starring Liam Neeson), and outlaw turned parliamentarian Peter Lalor.

South America was also another ripe landing ground for the Irish. The national hero of Chile is Bernardo O'Higgins whose paternal ancestors hailed from County Sligo. At the Battle of El Roble in 1813 O'Higgins led his men into combat with the cry: "Lads! Live with honor, or die with glory! He who is brave, follow me!"

You'd never know it from his name but the legendary Cuban revolutionary, Che Guevara, is a descendant of the Lynches of County Galway. Guevara's father proudly declared that "The first thing to note is that in my son's veins flowed the blood of the Irish rebels." And who can forget the quixotic members of the *Batallón de San Patricio*—the St. Patrick's Battalion—Irishmen who deserted the American army during the Mexican War to join their fellow Mexican Catholics.

But the Irish in their long diaspora, which continues to this day, put their major imprint on one country—the United States of

The Irish Diaspora: Taking a Part of Ireland with You | **61**

America. It is estimated that nearly fifty-seven million Americans can trace their ancestry to Ireland. The Irish have been here since before the birth of the American Republic. Charles Carroll was the only Irish-Catholic to sign the Declaration of Independence and since then the Irish have permeated every area of American life from politics, to sports, to Hollywood.

As they spread out across America they brought a little part of Ireland—the names of their towns, counties, and provinces—with them. Here is a sampling of how the Irish named America, bringing some of Ireland to the shores of North America, at least in name.

Cities and Towns

Everyone knows that Dublin is the capital of the Republic of Ireland, much loved for its cultural, revolutionary, and aesthetic beauty. When the Irish left their "Fair City" they did not forget it. In the United States there are at least twenty cities and towns named **Dublin**:

Dublin, Alabama; Dublin, Arizona; Dublin, Arkansas; Dublin, California; Dublin, North Carolina; Dublin, Florida; Dublin, Georgia; Dublin, Indiana; Dublin, Kentucky; Dublin, Maryland; Dublin, Michigan; Dublin, Mississippi; Dublin, New Hampshire; Dublin, New York; Dublin, Ohio; Dublin, Bucks County, Pennsylvania; Dublin, Fulton County, Pennsylvania; Dublin, Huntingdon County, Pennsylvania; Dublin, Texas; Dublin, Virginia

And the Irish from the North were not to be outdone either, naming five municipalities **Belfast**: Belfast, Maine; Belfast Township, Minnesota; Belfast, New York; Belfast, Pennsylvania; and Belfast Township, Pennsylvania.

Newry, County Down, is well represented: Newry, Maine; Newry Township, Freeborn County, Minnesota; Newry Township, Minnesota; Newry, Pennsylvania; Newry, South Carolina; Newry, Wisconsin

Derry, County Derry, is represented in the United States, apparently across sectarian lines. The Catholics have always called it "Derry" (from the Irish, *Doire*) and the Protestants refer to it as "Londonderry." However you declare it, it has made its way into American cartography: Derry, New Hampshire; Derry, Pennsylvania; Derry Township, Dauphin County, Pennsylvania; Derry Township, Mifflin County, Pennsylvania; Derry Township, Montour County, Pennsylvania; Derry Township, Westmoreland County, Pennsylvania

Londonderry: Londonderry, New Hampshire; Londonderry, Vermont; Londonderry Township, Bedford County, Pennsylvania; Londonderry Township, Chester County, Pennsylvania; Londonderry Township, Dauphin County, Pennsylvania

Provinces

There are four provinces of Ireland: Leinster (East), Munster (South), Connaught (West) and Ulster (North). Somehow Leinster and Connaught did not make it across the pond, but Munster and Ulster did:

Munster: Munster Township, Pennsylvania; Munster, Indiana; Munster, Texas

Ulster: Ulster Township, Iowa; Ulster County, New York; Ulster, New York; Ulster Township, Pennsylvania

Counties

There are thirty-two counties in Ireland, twenty-six in the Republic and six in Northern Ireland. (The Rev. Ian Paisley, mathematical genius, once famously declared that "Six into twenty-six will not go!") Sixteen counties of Ireland have found their way to America.

Antrim: Antrim, Louisiana; Antrim, New Hampshire; Antrim, New York; Antrim, Guernsey County, Ohio; Antrim Township, Wyandot County, Ohio; Antrim, Pennsylvania; Antrim County, Michigan; Antrim Township, Michigan; Antrim Township, Minnesota; Antrim Township, Pennsylvania

Armagh: Armagh, Pennsylvania; Armagh Township, Pennsylvania

Clare: Clare County, Michigan; Clare, Iowa; Clare, Michigan; Shannon County, Missouri; Shannon County, South Dakota (Shannon is a town in County Clare)

Donegal: Donegal, Pennsylvania

Fermanagh: Fermanagh Township, Pennsylvania

Galway: Galway (town), New York; Galway (village), New York

Kildare: Kildare Township, Minnesota; Kildare, Oklahoma; Kildare, Texas; Kildare, Wisconsin

Kilkenny: Kilkenny, Minnesota; Kilkenny, New Hampshire

Limerick: Limerick, Georgia; Limerick, Illinois; Limerick, Louisville; Limerick, Maine; Limerick, Mississippi; Limerick, New York; Limerick, Ohio; Limerick, South Carolina; Limerick Township, Pennsylvania; New Limerick, Maine

Mayo: Mayo, Florida

Monaghan: Monaghan Township, York County, Pennsylvania

Roscommon: Roscommon, Michigan; Roscommon County, Michigan

Sligo: Sligo, Missouri; Sligo, Pennsylvania

Tyrone: Tyrone, Colorado; Tyrone, Georgia; Tyrone Township, Franklin County, Illinois; Tyrone Township, Kent County, Michigan; Tyrone Township, Livingston County, Michigan; Tyrone, New Mexico; Tyrone, New York; Tyrone, Pennsylvania; Tyrone

Township, Adams County, Pennsylvania; Tyrone Township, Blair County, Pennsylvania; Tyrone Township, Perry County, Pennsylvania; Lower Tyrone Township, Fayette County, Pennsylvania; Upper Tyrone Township, Fayette County, Pennsylvania

Waterford: Waterford, Michigan; Waterford, New York; Waterford, Connecticut; Waterford, Ohio

Wexford: Wexford, Pennsylvania; Wexford, Toronto; Wexford County, Michigan; Wexford Creek, Wexford Township, Michigan

The Irish, always known for their wanderlust, have also managed to make their impression on, of all places, the planet **Mars**. There you'll find two craters: Louth and Wicklow.

12

THE ABBEY GOES
HOLLYWOOD:
THE SHIELDS BROTHERS AND
THE QUIET MAN

The motion picture that defines Ireland to many Irish-Americans is John Ford's *The Quiet Man*. Although made over sixty years ago, many still believe that the sentimental Ireland depicted in the film was the "real" Ireland of the time. It wasn't—and probably never was. The things about the movie that still resonate are those involved in it, especially its director, Irish-American John Ford, and two of its scene-stealing stars—Barry Fitzgerald and Arthur Shields.

Even today many don't realize that Barry (real name William Joseph Shields) and Arthur were brothers. Fitzgerald was born in 1888 on Walworth Street in the Portobello section of Dublin. (As a child he played with the younger siblings of James Joyce, who he called "a young man with a beard and very clever.") He was followed eight years later by his brother, Arthur. (Their house, right next to the Jewish Museum, is today marked by a plaque.) Their father, Adolphus, lists his occupation in the 1901 census as "press reader," but he was well-known in Dublin as a labor organizer. One of the big secrets of the family is that, although the brothers made their living in part playing Catholic priests, they were all Church of Ireland. (It should be noted that their mother, Fanny Sophia, who was born in Germany, lists her religion in the 1911 Census as "Agnostic." Their sister Madeline lists her religion as "Spiritualist"—very outspoken for women in early twentieth century Catholic Dublin!)

Arthur Shields has one of the great stories of twentieth century Ireland. He became involved early at the Abbey Theatre and worked there as actor, director, and stage manager. (He was known as "Boss" Shields.) But, unknown to many, he was also a patriot. In 1916 he was a member of the Irish Volunteers and was prepared to fight on Easter Sunday when the orders were countermanded. On Easter Monday the revolution was on again, and Shields went to the Abbey and retrieved his rifle from under the stage. He went around the corner to Liberty Hall and joined with James Connolly's Irish Citizen Army. (Connolly, an ardent socialist and master labor organizer, admired his father and congratulated Arthur on his parentage.) He then marched to the General Post Office in Sackville Street where he fought before evacuating on Friday. He was sent to Stafford Prison

Arthur Shields in The Fabulous Dorseys

in England with another famous rebel—Michael Collins—and from there they were both sent to the Frongoch internment camp in Wales. Both would return to Dublin by the end of 1916, Collins to terrorize the British and Shields to return to the Abbey stage.

William Shields—known as Will to his friends—worked in the Irish civil service in Dublin Castle, which must have been an interesting place during the War of Independence. After the Easter Rising he joined his brother at the Abbey and befriended a playwright by the name of Seán O'Casey. While Arthur, tall and lean, was the romantic star of the theatre, Barry Fitzgerald—he took the pseudonym because he was still working in the civil service while moonlighting as an actor—was short and quiet, but had a comic magic that today would be simply translated as "star power." Barry's relationship with O'Casey would soon have Ireland's foremost playwright writing parts for him, including Captain Boyle in *Juno and the Paycock* and Fluther Good in *The Plough and the Stars*. In fact, when that play premiered at the Abbey, riots broke out and little Barry was seen boxing outraged theatre-goers who attempted to take the stage.

In his wonderful book, *Hollywood Irish*, Adrian Frazier makes a very salient point about the two kinds of people—Catholic and Protestant—working at the Abbey. O'Casey, a Protestant, burst on the scene after the Irish Civil War with The *Shadow of the Gunman* and became the most prominent Irish playwright since John Millington Synge (also a Protestant). *Shadow* was followed by *Juno and the Paycock* and then *The Plough and the Stars*. *Plough* proved to be an incendiary play in the Dublin of its day. It questioned much of the nationalistic dogma of the time and brought an earthiness—it contained whores, drinkers, and looters—that upset much of the hierarchy in both government and Church.

It also created a chasm at the Abbey. The Catholic actors were very dubious and nervous about some of O'Casey's tenets as expressed in *Plough*, while the two Shields brothers sided with their friend O'Casey. This chasm turned into an open wound when the Abbey, under Yeats and Lady Gregory, rejected O'Casey's *The Silver Tassie*. The Shields brothers and O'Casey started to look for greener pastures. Fitzgerald and O'Casey found them in London, while Shields, for the moment, remained at the Abbey. But the (barely) state-subsidized Abbey was in terrible financial shape and it was decided that the Abbey Players would go on the road to America to keep the theatre afloat.

After the repressive, smothering atmosphere of Catholic Dublin in the new Irish Free State—Arthur Shields famously said that he didn't want to "say your prayers in Gaelic"—the United States seemed wonderful and invigorating. It also gave the Shields brothers a chance to make real money for the first time, something almost impossible in their itinerant trade back in Dublin. America also contained something called "Hollywood" and the lure would take several years, but finally seduced, first Barry, then Arthur. Both worked in John Ford's film version of *The Plough and the Stars*. While Arthur continued with the Abbey Players in many capacities, Barry stayed in Hollywood where after appearing in *Bringing Up Baby* with Cary Grant and Katherine Hepburn, he became a familiar face. The brothers would be reunited for Ford's *How Green Was My Valley* and *The Long Voyage Home.* With the advent of World War II, they were stuck in America and continued to work, mostly as reliable character actors.

Fitzgerald's big break came when he was cast as the ancient Father Fitzgibbons (although he was only fifty-six at the time) in *Going My Way.* To put it mildly, he stole the picture from Bing Crosby and was nominated for two Academy Awards, as Best Supporting Actor (which he won) and Best Actor (which Crosby won). (It's interesting to note the disparity in salary: Crosby was paid $150,000,

Barry Fitzgerald (William Joseph Shields) as Father Fitzgibbon in Going My Way

while Fitzgerald only pulled $8,750.) Fitzgerald's dual nominations forced the Academy to change the rules in that no one actor could be nominated in two categories for the same role. The Oscar made Fitzgerald a star and he went on to receive top billing in movies, including the seminal *Naked City* (1947). In this innovative Mark Hellinger production, filmed on the streets of New York in documentary style, Fitzgerald plays a tough New York homicide detective out to solve the murder of a model. For its time, the film is full of forensic science. The movie led to the television series *Naked City*, and without it there would be no *Law and Order* or *CSI*. In fact, Jerry Orbach's *Law and Order* detective Lennie Briscoe owes a lot to Fitzgerald's Lieutenant Dan Muldoon.

Fitzgerald made a lot of films—some pretty good, like *And Then There Were None* and *Union Station*, and some awful, like *Top o' the Morning*—between *Going My Way* and *The Quiet Man*. Shields meanwhile found steady character work in over thirty films and TV work during the same period. But John Ford's *The Quiet Man* was to be the apex of both their careers.

The Quiet Man remains one of the most beloved Irish-American films of all time, but it is interesting culturally as well. Fitzgerald plays the roguish matchmaker Michaleen Oge Flynn, while Shields plays the kindly Protestant minister, the Reverend Mister Cyril Playfair. Another Abbey player of renown, Eileen Crowe, plays Rev. Playfair's wife, while an Abbey up-and-comer by the name of Jack MacGowran made his movie debut, playing the fawning little squint, Ignatius Feeney.

The Quiet Man, ironically, represents a changing-of-the-acting-guard for the works of both Seán O'Casey and Samuel Beckett.

O'Casey wrote parts for Fitzgerald, which, in the years ahead, would be played by MacGowran. (MacGowran was on Broadway playing Fluther Good in *The Plough and the Stars* when he passed away from pneumonia in New York in 1973 at the age of fifty-four; his last movie part was in *The Exorcist*.) And in the years ahead MacGowran would become Samuel Beckett's favorite actor and Beckett would write parts specifically tailored to MacGowran's talents. "Author and actor are so commonly rooted in spirit," wrote Mel Gussow in the *New York Times* in 1970 about MacGowran's one man show, *Jack MacGowran in the Works of Samuel Beckett*, "that if Beckett were an actor he would be MacGowran, and if MacGowran were a writer he would be Beckett."

After *The Quiet Man* Fitzgerald's career tapered off, and he made only four more films and a few television appearances. He died in Dublin in 1961. Shields continued to work steadily, especially in television. His last film appearance was with Charlton Heston in *The Pigeon That Took Rome* in 1962. Unsurprisingly, he played a Vatican priest, Monsignor O'Toole. He died in 1970 in California. The Shields brothers are buried side-by-side in Deansgrange Cemetery, Blackrock, Dublin. Barry Fitzgerald headstone lists only his birth name, William J. Shields. Both, home at last.

13

HOLLYWOOD ON THE
LIFFEY:
THE IRISH FILM INDUSTRY—
BIGGER THAN YOU THINK

Ireland has always had a romance with movies going back almost to the time when Thomas Edison invented them. Dublin was packed with cinemas. In the late twentieth century, O'Connell Street counted many movie houses—the Carleton, the Capitol, the Metropole, the Ambassador, and the Savoy, the only one that survives. There were also cinemas on Middle Abbey Street, Granby Row (off Parnell Square), Eden Quay, Grafton Street, Camden Street, and even one on St. Stephen's Green West. In fact, James Joyce returned to Ireland in 1909 to try his hand at running the Volta Cinema on Mary Street, just blocks off O'Connell Street. Proving he was a writer and not a cinephile, Joyce's business collapsed. A plaque marks the spot of Joyce's entrepreneurial enterprise.

It seems most Irish-themed movies have emanated from Hollywood. But a great many of them, along with films about completely different topics, have come out of Ireland itself. One of the reasons was the establishment of Ardmore Studios in County Wicklow in 1958. And Ardmore, as strange as it may seem, has a rather odd connection to Michael Collins. Its first manager was Emmet Dalton, a man who served Collins as a general in the Free State Army during the Irish Civil War and who was with Collins the day he died in an ambush in County Cork. Additionally, Ardmore was opened by the then minister for industry and commerce—and future *Taoiseach*—Seán Lemass. Lemass was one of Collins's gunmen on Bloody Sunday 1920 when he was responsible for assassinating British secret service agents on Baggot Street in Dublin.

So the revolutionary fervor of Dalton and Lemass may have had something to do with one of the first films made there, *Shake Hands with the Devil,* in 1959. It starred James Cagney as a professor at the College of Surgeons who is secretly a commandant in the IRA. It was one of Cagney's last rolls before his early retirement, and he is superb as a twisted, misogynistic Republican die-hard. Michael Redgrave also has a small part as "The General," a thinly disguised portrait of Michael Collins.

Other films with nothing to do with Ireland made at Ardmore include *The Spy Who Came In from the Cold, The Blue Max, The*

Viking Queen, The Lion in Winter, Zardoz, The Last Remake of Beau Geste, and *Excalibur*. And there have been several films with Irish themes also filmed there, including *My Left Foot, The Commitments,* and *In the Name of the Father.*

My godmother, Mary Gallagher Edwards—a character straight out of O'Casey—recalled for me the making of John le Carré's *The Spy Who Came In from the Cold* in 1964, starring Richard Burton as British spy Alec Leamas (ironically the same last name as the Irish *Taoiseach* at the time, Seán Lemass, although spelled differently). Mary Edwards lived behind the Guinness Brewery, very near Marrowbone Lane and the Grand Canal. The stark contrast of the area apparently copied the dreariness of cold war Berlin. For the residents of this area, known as Maryland, it was not only an opportunity to ogle star Richard Burton, but also Elizabeth Taylor. "Everyone was out there," my godmother said, "waving at Dick and Liz!"

Among some of the other movies made in Ireland are John Huston's *Moby Dick, Educating Rita, Ulysses* (starring Milo O'Shea as Mr. Bloom), *Ryan's Daughter, Saving Private Ryan*, and *Quackser Fortune Has a Cousin in the Bronx*, an early Gene Wilder vehicle.

One destination that seemed to capture the imagination of auteurs is Kilmainham Gaol. Over a dozen movies have been filmed inside the sinister prison, including: *Michael Collins, The Wind That Shakes the Barley, In the Name of the Father, The Italian Job* (starring Michael Caine), *And No One Could Save Her* (starring Lee Remick), and Brendan Behan's *The Quare Fellow*.

Oscar No Stranger to Ireland

Twenty-eight. That's the number of Oscars Irish citizens have won.

Although only two Irish-born actors have won Oscars—**Barry Fitzgerald** for *Going My Way* and **Brenda Fricker** for *My Left Foot*—Oscar knows Ireland pretty well.

Daniel Day-Lewis has won three Oscars—*My Left Foot, There Will be Blood*, and *Lincoln*—and although born in England, he also holds Irish citizenship.

Four native-born Irishmen have been nominated, led by **Peter O'Toole**, nominated a whopping eight times: *Lawrence of Arabia; Becket; The Lion in Winter; Goodbye, Mr. Chips; The Ruling Class; The Stunt Man; My Favorite Year*, and *Venus*. O'Toole is followed by **Richard Harris** (*The Sporting Life* and *The Field*), **Stephen Rea** (*The Crying Game*), and **Liam Neeson** (*Schindler's List*).

Peter O'Toole in Lawrence of Arabia

Twelve Irish citizens have also won Oscars in various categories:

Cedric Gibbons won Best Art/Set Direction eleven times; **George Bernard Shaw** won Best Screenplay for *Pygmalion*, making him the only Irishman to win an Oscar and the Nobel Prize; **Michèle Burke** won two Oscars for Best Makeup: *Quest for Fire* and *Dracula*; **Josie McAvin**: shared Best Art Direction, *Out of Africa*; **Neil Jordan**: Best Original Screenplay, *The Crying Game*; **Peter O'Toole**: Honorary Oscar; **Corinne Marrinan**: Best Documentary Short, *A Note of Triumph*; **Martin McDonagh**: Best Short Film (Live Action): *Six Shooter*; **Glen Hansard**: shared Best Song, "Falling Slowly" from *Once*; **Richard Baneham**: (part of a team) Best Visual Effects, *Avatar*; and **Terry George** and **Oorlath George**: Best Short Film (Live Action): *The Shore*.

14

WHY THE IRISH LOVE
STATUES

I think it's safe to say that the Irish have a fixation on statues. In Dublin the streets and parks are clogged with them. Throughout the years there have been over seventy-five statues and monuments populating the streets of the Irish capital.

O'Connell Street is a prime example of this. At the south end of the thoroughfare sits Daniel O'Connell, the Liberator of Catholics in the nineteenth century. Dan is surrounded by busty angels, some of whom still bear the bullet scars on their bosoms from Ireland's rebellions.

To the north end stands "The Uncrowned King of Ireland," Charles Stewart Parnell, as portrayed by the brilliant Irish-American sculptor, Augustus Saint-Gaudens. The monument reads: "No Man has a right to fix the/Boundary to the march of a nation." Many a Dublin wag has noted that Parnell is pointing behind him at the Rotunda Maternity Hospital. Considering the carnal events surrounding the fall of Parnell, this juxtaposition of words and simultaneous gesticulation on Parnell's part has not gone unnoticed in by the natives.

And that may be just the reason why Dubliners love their statues—they get to comment on them and, better still, put words into their mouths.

Other statues in O'Connell Street include the architect of Irish self-prohibition—The Pledge—Father Matthew. Not far from him is a man who was a teetotaler—and one of the great labor organizers of his time—James Larkin. Facing the General Post Office at the foot of North Earl Street is the novelist James Joyce. He is perched against his walking stick and patiently poses for pictures with eager tourists. The locals, very aware of the great writer's predilection toward the drink and the whore, refer to him as "The Prick with the Stick."

James Joyce

Thomas Davis and Suds, College Green

Right by the GPO stands the Millennium Spire. The Spire stands in the exact place where Nelson's Pillar stood for 158 years before being blown up by the IRA in 1966. This event, it is said, made Lord Horatio Nelson Ireland's first astronaut. (His lonely, dismembered head can be viewed at the Pearse Street Library, two blocks from Pearse Station at Westland Row.) Lord Nelson's fate has been met by other icons of the British occupier—statues of both King George II and William of Orange were also blown up. Queen Victoria's statue met a more ironic fate—like many Irishmen under her reign, she was poetically exiled to Australia where she is currently on display in Sydney.

As one crosses O'Connell Bridge and enters Westmoreland Street, the first statue is that of poet and song writer Thomas Moore, famous for his "The Meetings of the Waters." Moore's statue sits atop a former public lavatory, which prompted Leopold Bloom to comment in Joyce's *Ulysses*: "They did right to put him up over a urinal: meeting of the waters."

A few paces away is the front gate of Trinity College, stoically guarded by the statues of alumni Oliver Goldsmith and Edmund

Molly Malone

Burke. And just up College Green opposite the Bank of Ireland is Edward Delaney's statue of Thomas Davis, nationalist and author of "A Nation Once Again." There is a fountain surrounding Davis, and it has become a popular pastime for Trinity students to pour in detergent, creating a bubbly mess and making this the cleanest statue in all of Dublin.

Maybe the most popular statue in Dublin is voluptuous Molly Malone at the corner of Grafton and Suffolk Streets. Tourists love to be photographed with her bosoms, not to mention her cockles and mussels as well. To one and all, she is "The Tart with the Cart."

The advance up Grafton Street brings us to St. Stephen's Green, which is guarded by the Fusiliers' Arch which commemorates all those who fought for Britain in the Boer War. To Dubliners it is simply, "The Traitor's Gate." The Green itself is populated with busts, which as you can see, in many forms, seems to be a preoccupation with

Close-up of Great Famine statue

the Irish: Joyce again is represented, as are the Countess Marki-evicz, who commanded this park during the Easter Rising, Jeremiah O'Donovan Rossa, the incorrigible old Fenian, and United Irishman patriot Robert Emmet, who declared from the dock before execution in 1803: "Let no man write my epitaph . . . until my country takes her place among the nations of the earth . . ."

Outside the Green, not far from the Shelbourne Hotel, is another Edward Delaney statue, the imposing figure of Theobald Wolfe Tone, one of the leaders of the 1798 rebellion. In 1971 Protestant militants blew up poor Wolfe Tone and he had to be taken in, said the locals, to have his genitalia resoldered.

Not far from the Green is Merrion Square, home to genius such as W.B. Yeats, George Russell, and Oscar Wilde. In fact, across the street from the house Wilde grew up in is one of the most outrageous statues in Dublin—a colorful Wilde comically and lewdly laid out on a boulder. He is known to one and all as "The Quare in the Square." Not that far away in the square there is a bust of Michael Collins, the greatest Irish statesman, whose revolutionary genius helped create today's Irish Republic.

There are other statues around Dublin town dedicated to the memories of writer Brendan Behan, poet Patrick Kavanagh, patriot James Connolly, fatigued shoppers (the frequently mocked "Hags with the Bags" on the north end of the Ha'penny Bridge), and the victims of the Great Famine. All have a story—and every Dubliner is eager to tell you his version of it.

15
GAY GAELS

E very St. Patrick's Day, inevitably, the old debate will be renewed. Should gays be banned from the St. Patrick's Day Parade? (Note: New York City has finally relented, but Boston remains steadfast in their prohibition.) The Church—which has had more than their share of gay problems—the Ancient Order of Hibernians, and other like-minded organizations will band together, think back fondly on their nineteenth century prejudices, and shout an authoritarian "NYET!" There will be all kinds of excuses ("Gays can march, but they can't do so under a banner"), but everyone knows the real reason. The one word answer is "prejudice."

It's ironic that this bigotry towards gays should remain so prevalent today, since Ireland's history has been enriched, yesterday and today, by its gay members. And you don't have to look too hard for great examples—two of the sixteen men executed by the British in 1916 were most likely gay—Sir Roger Casement (definitely) and Pádraig Pearse (probably latently). Oscar Wilde was hounded to his grave because he flaunted Victorian law and convention. (Ironically, both Casement and Wilde would be pursued and prosecuted, Inspector Javert-style, by Sir Edward Carson, the less than patriotic Orange bigot.)

Two of Ireland's most well known writers, Oscar Wilde and Brendan Behan, have more than their occupation and city of birth in common—both were bisexual. People forget that Wilde, one of the great flamboyant characters of all time, had a wife and fathered two children before his tragic fall. Behan's image of ex-IRA man, saloon-loving icon-

Brendan Behan

oclast, contrasts almost violently with his affection for young boys, revealed first by Ulick O'Connor in his Behan biography, *Brendan*. Despite having a devoted wife and fathering a child, Behan's homosexuality, which first blossomed when he was serving time in a British borstal for young boys, frightened and disturbed him until his premature death in 1964.

Micheál Mac Liammóir, who along with his lover Hilton Edwards, founded the Gate Theatre in 1928. (The famous Dublin line about what separated the Gate and Abbey Theatres—"It's the difference between Sodom and Begorra"—may also have referred to Mac Liammóir's sexual preference.) He was known for his openly gay and flamboyant lifestyle. His film works included Iago in Orson Welles's *Othello*, the narrator of *Tom Jones*, and the part of Sweet Alice in John Huston's *The Kremlin Letter*. On stage his one-man show about Oscar Wilde, *The Importance of Being Oscar*, was critically

acclaimed. He claimed to have had a homosexual relationship with General Eoin O'Duffy, one-time head of the *Garda Síochána*, the Irish police force. He died in 1978.

Thomas MacGreevy was a poet, critic, and a friend to both Joyce and Beckett in Paris. He was also director of National Gallery of Ireland in Dublin. In his book, *Samuel Beckett: The Last Modernist*, Anthony Cronin wrote "It might be accurate to say that his [Beckett's] relationship with MacGreevy had, though it was not sexual, an element of the homo-erotic in it, as indeed some of Beckett's later relationships were to have." MacGreevy died in 1967.

In recent years other Irish writers have come out and declared their homosexuality, most prominently novelist

David Norris

Colm Tóibín and Nuala O'Faolain, who

wrote about her relationship with Nell McCafferty in *Are You Some-body*? But there was a legal fight ahead that would shock, nudge, and then shove Ireland into the twenty-first century.

Twenty-First Century? This Way

"We were the most conservative revolutionaries in history."

Those are the words of Kevin O'Higgins, one of the architects of the modern Irish state and one of the most controversial figures in Irish history. What he might have been talking about is how after 700 years of occupation and a bloody six-year revolution, the Irish adopted most British laws verbatim. Revolution is supposed to be for change. Apparently for the Irish, just a change in administrator was needed because the British laws were, well, swell.

So The Offenses Against the Person Act 1861 (in the vernacular, the anti-buggery act) and The Criminal Law of Amendment of 1885 (the gross indecency act)—laws written by the English—remained on the law books of the Republic of Ireland up until the 1980s.

Enter David Norris. Norris is an Irish Senator and a Joyce scholar. He is also openly gay. He challenged the law in the Irish Supreme Court and lost. He then brought his case to the European Court of Human Rights (basically suing his own country in Norris v. Ireland) and finally won in 1988. At last, both laws were repealed in 1993.

So, finally, on gay rights at least, Ireland has been brought into the light of the twenty-first century. Dublin every June has its own Gay Pride Parade and many of the partiers end up at The George, Dublin's foremost gay bar on South Great Georges Street, to continue the celebration.

Brendan Behan wrote a poem about the death of Oscar Wilde in which he said *"No Pernod to brace him/Only holy water."* You just know that if Oscar Wilde were around today he'd be sipping his Pernod Absinthe, straight, at the bar of The George. And I think Brendan might join him.

16
ÉIRE ERRS ON CENSORSHIP

J ames J. "Jimmy" Walker, the mayor of New York City during the Roaring Twenties and one of the great Irish political rogues of all time, once famously declared, "I never knew a girl who was ruined by a book." It was advice that the nascent Irish Free State should have heeded, but didn't.

If there's one thing that Ireland is immensely proud of, it is its writers. Bridges over the River Liffey have been named for O'Casey, Joyce, and Beckett. Statues of her hero writers abound in Dublin; Joyce, Wilde, Patrick Kavanagh, and Brendan Behan are all prominently located. Ireland's literary history has become a prime source of revenue as a tourist attraction. In Dublin alone there is the Writer's Museum on Parnell Square, the nearby Joyce Centre on North Georges Street, the George Bernard Shaw Museum on Synge Street and, of course, one of the great places of literature—Joyce's Martello Tower overlooking Dublin Bay in Sandycove.

What is forgotten is that many famous writers left Ireland in disgust—Joyce, Wilde, Shaw, Beckett, and O'Casey; Shaw famously declared: "I showed my appreciation of my native land in the usual way—by getting out of it as soon as I possibly could."

Despite that statement, Shaw, an independent thinker and a man with strong nationalist feelings, wrote in *Mrs. Warren's Profession* that "All censorships exist to prevent anyone from challenging current conceptions and existing institutions. All progress is initiated by challenging current conceptions, and executed by supplanting existing institutions. Consequently, the first condition of progress is the removal of censorship."

In *The Picture of Dorian Gray*, Oscar Wilde sagaciously wrote, "The books that the world calls immoral are the books that show the world its own shame." Eugene O'Neill, a tortured Irish soul if there ever was one, was more blunt: "Censorship of anything, at any time, in any place, on whatever pretense, has always been and always will be the last resort of the boob and the bigot."

One of the reasons for the animosity of its writers was Ireland's preoccupation with censorship. Working hand-in-hand with the Catholic Church, soon after the establishment of the Irish Free State in 1922, was the appointment of the "Committee on Evil Literature"—which sounds like a concoction from Monty Python.

Not satisfied with only a "Committee on Evil Literature," the state established The Censorship of Publications Acts of 1929, which created the Censorship of Publications Board. And they were a busy bunch, banning such writers as Liam O'Flaherty, Seán O'Faoláin, Francis Stuart, Oliver St. John Gogarty, Frank O'Connor, Benedict Kiely, Honoré de Balzac, Aldous Huxley, J.D. Salinger, and Brendan Behan. Apparently, not wanting to appear sexist, they banned two of Edna O'Brien's novels, *The County Girls* and *The Lonely Girl*, the former because Dublin Archbishop John Charles McQuaid thought it "particularly bad."

Prior to the twin O'Brien bannings, McQuaid had been involved in O'Casey pulling his play, *The Drums of Father Ned*, from the 1958 Dublin Theatre Festival. In order to give his blessing McQuaid had requested "certain structural alterations," which O'Casey refused. This outrage prompted Samuel Beckett to withdraw three plays of his own from the festival: *Act Without Words I* and *II* and *Krapp's Last Tape*. Beckett was particularly incensed at the Catholic Church and the meekness of its followers. Several years later, he bitterly observed of the Church: "They have buggered us into glory!"

The late twentieth century finally brought some sanity to Ireland's Victorian fixations. Today there are but eight books banned in Ireland and these books deal with abortion and sex, something Ireland's banned writers would still probably find incredulous. As of today there are no books banned in Ireland because of either indecency or obscenity. Perhaps as a reward, UNESCO designated Dublin a City of Literature in 2010.

Perhaps Ireland, long ago, should have heeded the words of another Irish-American author and winner of the Pulitzer Prize: "Let us welcome controversial books and controversial authors." Wise words, compliments of one John F. Kennedy.

17

WHAT'S A *TAOISEACH*?
HOW THE IRISH
GOVERNMENT HAS
EVOLVED SINCE 1916

ne word that is heard daily in Ireland in the media and in conversation and flummoxes visitors is *Taoiseach* (pronounced Tee-shuck). *An Taoiseach* is the title of the Irish prime minister. It is the Irish word for "chief" or "leader."

The Republic of Ireland employs a parliamentary system, strangely fashioned after the one cherished by their ancient enemy, the English. Over the years this system has been tweaked on several occasions.

At the Easter Rising of 1916 Pádraig Pearse was declared the "President of the Provisional Government." He was shot by the British four days after his surrender.

Undeterred by this turn of events, the Irish returned to their revolution-making and in the general election following the end of the Great War in 1918 elected their own parliament, seated in Dublin and called *Dáil Éireann*. Éamon de Valera, the last surviving commandant of the Easter Rising, was duly appointed *Príomh Aire*, first minister or prime minister, of the new *Dáil*. Shortly thereafter de Valera left for a twenty-month tour of the United States of America where he introduced himself not as *Príomh Aire*, but as the august "President of the Irish Republic." Meanwhile, back in Dublin, the revolution went on under the guidance of the greatest guerrilla warrior of the twentieth century, Michael Collins.

After the Treaty negotiations the government had another shake-up, and the man now running the show, W.T. Cosgrave (after the successive deaths of Arthur Griffith and Collins in August 1922), was known as the "president of the executive council." Cosgrave was succeeded by Éamon de Valera in 1932, and in 1937 President de Valera, in a very complicated maneuver, restructured the government (this also included the resurrection of the recently decommissioned *Seanad*, or senate, the

Éamon de Valera

upper chamber to the *Dáil*). The head of this new government became the *Taoiseach*.

In the history of Ireland there have been twelve *Taoisigh* (the plural of *Taoiseach*):

Éamon de Valera (1937–48; 1951–54; 1957–59); John A. Costello (1948–51; 1954–57); Seán Lemass (1959–66); Jack Lynch (1966–73; 1977–79); Liam Cosgrave (1973–77); Charles Haughey (1979–81; 1982; 1987–92); Garret FitzGerald (1981–82; 1982–87); Albert Reynolds (1992–94); John Bruton (1994–1997); Bertie Ahern (1997–2008); Brian Cowen (2008–2011); Enda Kenny (2011–present)

At the time he changed the constitution in 1937, de Valera also established the new office of president of Ireland. The most important duty of the new president was to be head of state. The duties of the Irish president closely resemble those of the British monarch. The first president was the founder of the Gaelic League, Douglas Hyde. He was followed by Seán T. O'Kelly, de Valera himself, Erskine H. Childers, Cearbhall Ó Dálaigh, and Patrick Hillery.

The office of president came to be a resting place for rusted politicians for de Valera's party, *Fianna Fáil.* This continued until 1990 when Mary Robinson of the Labour Party won the presidency in an upset. At that time Mrs. Robinson said, "I was elected . . . above all by the women of Ireland—*Mna na hÉireann*—who instead of rocking the cradle rocked the system and who came out massively to make their mark on the ballot paper and on a new Ireland."

President Robinson was succeeded by Mary McAleese. The current president is Michael D. Higgins, elected in 2011.

Mary Robinson

18
NIGHTTOWN:
"THE WHORES WILL BE BUSY"

Surprisingly, today much of James Joyce's Dublin of *Ulysses* is extant. True, some addresses have gone missing, like Leopold Bloom's home at 7 Eccles Street, but many of the buildings and public monuments remain. However, one neighborhood has totally disappeared—Nighttown is no more.

Nighttown was Dublin's erstwhile red light district. (It was also known as "Monto" after Montgomery Street, or the "Kips.") It was made famous by James Joyce in *Ulysses*, in Episode 15, "Circe." Nighttown was located in the triangular area north of the Customs House, up to Mountjoy Square, and then east to the area around Amien Street railroad depot (now Connolly Station).

Becky Cooper and Friends

In Circe, Joyce's duo heroes, Stephen Dedalus and Leopold Bloom, find themselves at Bella Cohen's whorehouse. It is believed that

Bella was fashioned after a real-life Dublin madam by the name of Becky Cooper who serviced the area, literally, from the 1890s through the 1920s. She was so famous that there was even a little ditty written (supposedly by Oliver St. John Gogarty) about her:

> Italy's maids are fair to see
> And France's maids are willing,
> But less expensive, 'tis to me,
> Becky's for a shilling."

Amazingly, one hundred years after her heyday Becky is still remembered. The Dubliners' Ronnie Drew gave her—along with other madams like May Oblong and Mary Wong—a shout-out in their song about another Nighttown whore, Dicey Reilly.

Joyce and his friend (and later foe) Gogarty, the avatar for "Stately plump Buck Mulligan" in *Ulysses*, were among Becky's regulars, and Gogarty even wrote a limerick commemorating the whoring enterprise of the young Joyce:

There is a young fellow named Joyce
Possessed of a sweet tenor voice,
He goes down to the kips
With a song on his lips,
And biddeth the harlots rejoice.

Nighttown served many pious Dubliners and even a future King—Edward VII. (Edward, as the Prince of Wales, was an aficionado of whores and had a regular one in Paris on his payroll. Supposedly, after a fight with her, he exclaimed "I've paid you enough money over the years to build a battleship!" to which she replied, "And you've pumped enough semen into me to float it!") But probably the biggest clientele of the Kips were the soldiers of the British army and the sailors of the Royal Navy (the docks were only blocks away). By 1900 it was estimated that there was as many as 1,600 prostitutes working in Nighttown. Dublin had many military barracks—the British, for good reason, never fully trusted the insurrection-minded locals—and the big Curragh military camp in County Kildare was only thirty miles away. So the area was flooded with the military. In fact, Stephen in Circe's gets into an altercation with a British soldier while in Nighttown.

Ulysses takes place in 1904 just after a flood of soldiers had returned to Dublin following the conclusion of the Second Boer War in 1902. (The Dubliners in their wonderful folksong about Nighttown, "Monto," nailed it when they called the Dublin Fusiliers dirty old "bamboozeleers.") In fact Gogarty, in one of the great literary pranks of the time, published a poem in "honor" of the returning soldiers and what it meant to Dublin. He called it "Ode to Welcome":

The Gallant Irish yeoman,
Home from the war has come
Each victory gained o'er foeman,
Why should our bards be dumb?

How shall we sing their praises
Or glory in their deeds?
Renowned their worth amazes,
Empire their prowess needs.

So to Old Ireland's hearts and homes
We welcome now our own brave boys
In cot and ball; 'neath lordly domes
Love's heroes share once more our joys.

Love is the Lord of all just now,
Be he the husband, lover, son,
Each dauntless soul recalls the vow
By which not fame, but love was won.

United now in fond embrace
Salute with joy each well-loved face,
Yeoman, in women's hearts you hold the place."

If you take the first letter from the first word of each line you'll truly know what the returning Boer War veterans meant to Dublin: "The whores will be busy."

Shankers Ryan

Nighttown and a relative of Becky Cooper also played a role in one of the most sordid events in Irish revolutionary history.

Becky Cooper had a brother named John "Shankers" Ryan, who, during the War of Independence, was a British tout and spy. On the evening of Saturday, November 20, 1920, he trailed Dick McKee and Peadar Clancy, the commandant and vice-commandant of the Dublin Brigades of the IRA, back to their residence at 36 Lower Gloucester Street. McKee and Clancy were making final plans for the mission that would happened at 9 a.m. the following morning—Bloody Sunday—when Michael Collins's private squad, the Twelve Apostles, would assassinate the entire British secret service in Dublin.

Shankers tipped off the authorities at Dublin Castle and McKee and Clancy were apprehended. They would be beaten to death the following day by the British in revenge. Collins soon found out who was responsible for the capture of McKee and Clancy—one Shankers Ryan—and made note.

He did not strike until the morning of Saturday, February 5, 1921, when the Squad caught up to Shankers as he bellied up to the bar at Hynes Pub in Lower Gloucester Street for his daily eye-opener. They shot Ryan dead where he stood, sending a clear message from Michael Collins—"Spies Beware"—to any other eager touts in Nighttown who would seek employment from the British occupiers.

Nighttown, Hollywood Style

One wonders how much the assassination of Shankers Ryan and the hijinks of the British and IRA in Nighttown had on writer Liam O'Flaherty. He located his novel, *The Informer*, within the confines of Nighttown. John Ford went on to make *The Informer* into a classic 1935 film, starring Victor McLaglen, who won the Academy Award for Best Actor, while the film itself garnered three Academy Awards of its own.

Another film that darkly explores the world of Dublin's whores and pimps is *Shake Hands with the Devil* starring James Cagney, made on location in Dublin in 1959. Cagney—think a misogynistic Cody Jarrett in *White Heat*, only with a brogue—plays a professor at the Royal College of Surgeons who is secretly a commandant in the IRA. After one of his students is shot by the British he is called to a flat—in Nighttown?—where he confronts a whore and her pimp and warns them to get out of the business and steer clear of the IRA. In the background can be heard the screech of a locomotive. Perhaps a train heading into Amien Street station?

The Legion of Mary to the Rescue

Although Nighttown is recalled primarily for its colorful whoring past, it should be noted that many decent, hardworking people lived there, many of them living in absolute poverty and disease because of appalling sanitary conditions. Many a poor family relocated there as the neighborhood transitioned from wealthy enclave to ghetto in the years following the Great Famine.

With the establishment of the Irish Free State in 1922, something dramatic happened to Nighttown—all the British servicemen left, severely affecting carnal commerce. The new Free State took on a new pious façade as the state and church (Nighttown is, ironically, part of the parish of the city's Catholic Pro-Cathedral on Marlborough Street) collaborated to regulate the morals of the gentry. This was the death knell for Nighttown.

A man by the name of Frank Duff formed the Legion of Mary in Dublin in 1921. Duff—who was briefly secretary to Michael Collins in 1922—took an interest in the whores of Dublin and when he found out what atrocious conditions they lived in he moved heaven and earth to rid Nighttown of them. For as long as there was a Nighttown the police—through both bribery and indifference—paid it no heed. But by the Lenten season of 1925, Duff had the police force of the new state on his side. Almost all the whores and madams were cleared out by the police under the command of Colonel Dave Neligan, chief superintendent of the detective branch. It was another Collins connection because Neligan, during the revolution, was famously the "Spy in the Castle," part of Collins's extensive spy network.

Over the years urban renewal took place as public housing was built for the inhabitants. They even went so far as

James Joyce

to change the names of the streets, as if changing the names could protect the innocent.

Notorious Montgomery Street morphed into Foley Street. Gloucester Street became Seán MacDiarmada Street. Mecklenburgh Street became Tyrone Street, then Railway Street. And in the irony of ironies Mabbot Street became Corporation Street, and then as the millennium approached it was renamed for one of Nighttown's most famous clients and publicists—James Joyce Street, neatly tucked in between Railway and Foley Streets. Joyce would probably think it the perfect salute from his native city.

There is one odd renaming that didn't quite get the respectability memo—Little Martin's Lane was curiously rebranded Beaver Street. Maybe Becky Cooper got the last laugh.

19
HOW THE IRISH PUT THE "E" IN WHISKEY

Not surprisingly, the Irish invented whiskey. They called it, in the Irish, *uisce beatha*—the "water of life." The English, mystified at the happiness of the locals and their magical water—pronounced "ish-key-baha"—tasted it, liked it, and declared it "whiskey."

Today all Irish whiskeys are spelled with an "E." However different whiskeys from different countries may or may not have an "E" in their particular spellings of whiskey.

Take, for example, the United States. Most American whiskeys—Bourbon, Tennessee, Corn, Rye, Malt, Wheat—use the "E" in their version of whiskey. (There are exceptions: Old Forester, Maker's Mark, George Dickel, and Rittenhouse, among them.) This may be explained in that most of the people who settled in the southern and Appalachian parts of colonial America in the eighteenth century were Scotch Orange Protestants from the Ulster province of Ireland. So it would be natural for them to take along the version of "whiskey" they were familiar with. In America they would be known as "Scotch-Irish," but to many of their Catholic countrymen they would always be "hillbillies"—people from the hills who were the followers of William of Orange, King Billy, thus "billy boys." (King Billy is still derided by Ireland's Catholics, as one ditty reminds us: *"Up the long ladder and down the short rope, to hell with King Billy and God bless the Pope!"*) The only Protestant and Catholic common denominator seemed to be their adherence to the "E" in their whiskeys.

Just across the sea in Scotland, there is no "E" in their Scotch whisky. There are theories as to why the Irish have an "E" in their whiskey and the Scotch do not. One is how their individual Gaelic words for water are pronounced.

The Irish *uisce* is pronounced "ish-key" and the Scotch *uisge* is pronounced "oosh-ka"

In Canada there is no "E" in their whisky. The same is true of Australia where they produce single malt whiskies. This is surprising because so much of Australia was populated with Irish, many of whom went involuntarily as revolutionary felons. India followed their British occupiers and failed to adopt an "E" for their whisky, as did both Japan and Germany.

There seems to be one simple rule—Germany being the lone exception—for remembering if there is an "E" in your favorite whiskey: 1) if your favorite booze's country of origin has an "E" in it—like Ireland—it's WhiskEy; 2) if it doesn't, it's just plain old Whisky.

Regardless, *Sláinte.*

20

SEARCHING UNDER THE OULD SOD FOR YOUR IRISH GENEALOGICAL ROOTS

Twenty years ago, when my mother died in New York, I returned to Dublin to bury her in Glasnevin Cemetery. I stood in the bleak November damp and looked at the family gravestone, which had the names of my maternal grandparents and two of my uncles. Suddenly I realized I really didn't know very much about my own family. My mother's family had been destroyed by disease and then revolution, which resulted in my mother spending a decade of her youth in an orphanage. I took a photograph of the headstone—which recorded death dates—and asked a cousin to see if she could get me their death certificates.

From there the adventure took off, especially with the advent and help of the Internet. I've traced my family tree on both sides as far back as the great-grandparents and, in one instance, to my maternal great-great-grandmother—she lived smack in the middle of "Nighttown," James Joyce's red light district in *Ulysses*. It took a lot of hard work on both sides of the Atlantic, a lot of hits-and-misses, but finally I have been able to paste together a portrait of my father's family in rural County Louth and my mother's family, proud southsiders in Dublin City.

Here's how you can do it too.

The most important step is in the preparation. The more information you have—such as full names and birth/death/marriage dates—the easier your search will be. But you can also start with very basic information such as a name and a date of birth. Gather as many materials as you can (i.e., birth/baptismal/marriage/death certificates; passports/travel documents/green cards/citizenship papers). If you don't know how your family got to America, a good start would be to go to a paid website like Ancestry.com and scour American census records, or go to the free Ellis Island website (Ellisisland.org) and check out incoming passengers lists to the United States. Then start working backwards.

Certificate Nuggets

What will you find in Irish birth/death/marriage certificates besides the obvious? Tiny genealogical nuggets! For instance, on birth certificates you'll find addresses and occupations. Death certificates will also supply addresses and people who were present

Ellis Island

at the time of death. Marriage certificates will supply maiden names, occupations, plus the names of the bride and groom's fathers and their occupations. The discoveries on one certificate can lead to ten future searches!

Step One: The Irish Censuses of 1901 and 1911

The National Archives of Ireland provides many important services—all of them FREE!

Foremost among these services is the Censuses of 1901 and 1911, administered by the British government. You can access both censuses at: http://www.census.nationalarchives.ie/. All counties, including those of Northern Ireland, are included.

These are the last two remaining intact censuses of Ireland while the country was occupied by the British. For some reason, during World War I, nineteenth century Irish censuses between 1861 and 1891 were pulped. (The National Archives has, however, recently posted surviving census fragments and substitutes for 1821, 1831, 1841, and 1851.) The 1921 census—the last conducted by the British government before independence—was largely lost when the IRA set fire to the Customs House in Dublin in May 1921.

The information provided includes names, addresses, occupations, religion—the two most popular designations are Church of Ireland (COI) and Roman Catholic (RC)—literacy ("can read and write"), whether Gaelic (referred to as "Irish" in Ireland) is spoken, and number of children born alive. The form is signed by the head of the household, perhaps giving you a first look at the penmanship of your great-great-grandfather.

Step Two: Parish Records

Another invaluable service provided by the National Archives is the Parish Records, with free access available at: http://www.irishgenealogy.ie/. (This site also makes other valuable links available, including those to Irish and British military sites and land and registry deeds, among others.)

Parish records include baptismal information and, to a lesser extent, marriage and death information. Currently available are Carlow (COI), Cork and Ross (RC), Dublin (COI, PRESBY, RC), and Kerry (COI, RC). Updates are ongoing. It is also possible, in certain circumstances, to print out the actual page about the baptism or marriage.

The National Library of Ireland (http://www.nli.ie/en/genealogy-advisory-service.aspx; located in Dublin at 2/3 Kildare Street, just down the street from the Shelbourne Hotel) offers microfilm copies of Catholic Parish Registers and the Tithe Applotment Books and online access to Griffiths Primary Valuation of Property and many printed resources such as newspapers and trade directories.

The Genealogy Advisory Service is available free of charge to all personal callers to the library who wish to research their family history in Ireland. (Check website for seasonal hours and other genealogical services.)

Another excellent, free service is provided by the Mormon Church. It's called Family Search (https://www.familysearch.org/) and they refer to themselves as "The World's Largest Genealogy Organization." It is through this service that I found the birth and death dates of many of my relatives, which I later turned into birth/death/marriages certificates in Dublin.

If you are visiting the rural areas of Ireland, it is quite possible to go to the local parish house and ask to review their baptismal and marriage records.

Step Three: Cemeteries

If you know where your people are buried, cemeteries contain a wealth of family information, specifically birth and death dates on headstones. More detailed information can often be found in records located in cemetery offices.

My mother's family is buried in Glasnevin Cemetery in Dublin. The newly built Glasnevin Trust Museum offers a fascinating look at Ireland's foremost cemetery (take a taxi or 9 bus from the City Centre and ask the driver to let you out near the cemetery). The daily tour includes entrance into Daniel O'Connell's tomb (it is considered "lucky" to touch his coffin), a visit to the appropriately named "Republican Plot" where many famous Irish revolutionaries are buried, plus visits to the graves of patriots Éamon de Valera and Michael Collins.

But the biggest service offered by the Glasnevin Trust is its fantastic website (http://glasnevintrust.ie/), which gives access to the names of almost all who have been buried at Glasnevin from 1828 to the present. A preliminary search is *free* and a detailed search of the grave is available for a small fee.

This service is invaluable because it will provide you a list of *everyone* in a particular grave. Often, names were not recorded on the headstone

Step Four: General Register Office Research Room

The bad news is that GRO Research Room is not Internet friendly (only rudimentary information is available at: http://www.groireland. ie/research.htm). The good news is that if you go there they have all the information you'll ever need. Nothing is on the Internet; you'll have to search in person through dog-eared index books.

How to find it: The General Register Office Research Room is located on Werburgh Street, near Christ Church Cathedral. It is difficult to find. On the corner of Werburgh Street opposite Christ Church is the Lord Edward Restaurant. Cross the street to St. Werburgh's Protestant Church where Lord Edward Fitzgerald is buried. To the right of the church is the parish house. To the right of the parish house is an alley. At the end of this alley is the General Register Office Research Room. Hours are daily, 9:30 a.m. to 4:30 p.m. Finding this place is the most difficult obstacle. Once inside, you will have access to all births/deaths/marriages in Ireland from 1864 onward (non-Catholic marriages from 1845).

It is not cheap, but reasonable for the information provided: about €20 for a day-long search of all the indexes (particular search is €2). Once you find your relative, there is a €4 certificate photocopy fee with a maximum of five photocopies per person per day. Staff is extremely professional and helpful. Your photocopy will be brought to you within ten minutes. Instant genealogical gratification!

The Jigsaw of Genealogy—Guinness Archives to the Rescue

Searching for family—especially family that may have lived and died in Ireland over one hundred years ago—can be frustrating. Patience is the greatest virtue. Every relative you find adds to the jigsaw puzzle. One name leads to another. An example is my great-uncle Charlie Conway, who, until several years ago, I had never heard of. Here's how I found Uncle Charlie, my maternal grandmother's colorful, oldest brother:

1. My great-grandmother, Mary Anne Conway, according to the 1901 census, lived at 26 Temple Lane. By the 1911 census she

was no longer there. At the General Register Office I searched for deaths between 1901 and 1911. I found my great-granny had died in 1909. On the death certificate it stated that her son, Charles Conway, was present at the time of her death. It also gave Charlie's address.

2. I found Charlie at that address in the 1911 census. He stated that his occupation was "brewery policeman." This piqued my interest and I got in touch with the highly-efficient people at the Guinness Archive (http://www.guinness-storehouse.com/en/GenealogySearch.aspx). Within twenty-four hours they reported back to me that Charlie had indeed been a Guinness employee between 1902 and 1932. I also found out that during World War I Charlie was a corporal in the Royal Field Artillery of the British army. He is listed in Guinness's honor roll of employees who served in His Majesty's Naval, Military, and Air Forces, 1914–1918. If you are a blood relative Guinness will allow you to view your relative's personnel file. The Guinness Archives are located at the Guinness Storehouse—which, ironically, was Uncle Charlie's beat—off James's Street, the same building where the Guinness tour is conducted.

Irish in the British Military

The Royal Dublin Fusiliers Association (www.greatwar.ie) is a valuable resource service run by Seán Connolly about the erstwhile Royal Dublin Fusiliers. The British Army WWI regiment was one of the five Irish regiments disbanded by the British following the

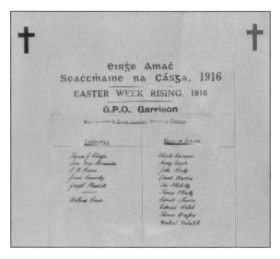

The Roll of Honour of 1916 Easter Rising

signing of the treaty in December 1921, which created the Irish Free State. Through this website I found that my Uncle Charlie joined the British army in 1885 before being cashiered in 1901. He returned to active service—at the age of forty-five—at the outbreak of the Great War in 1914 before being cashiered out again in 1918.

There's an old joke that Irish-Americans will pay $1,000 to someone to find their Irish roots. Then when they find out what rogues their ancestors were they end up paying the same person $10,000 to keep the family secrets.

Save yourself some money—do it yourself!

ST. FINIAN WAS BORN 454 A.D.
HE WAS EDUCATED BY ST. DAVID IN WALES
HE FOUNDED HIS MONASTERY
AT CLONARD,
AND DIED 12TH DECEMBER 563.

21
SAINTLY IRISH NAMES

One of the most startling changes in Ireland in the last thirty years is how the Irish have reverted to using more Irish names for their offspring.

As was discussed in Chapter 3: Name that Irish Pejorative, the Irish in the nineteenth and twentieth centuries had a tendency to give their children English names (a random check of the Irish Census of 1901 or 1911 at http://www.census.nationalarchives.ie/ will corroborate this). There was Michael (Mick) and Patrick (Paddy) and Tim and Tom and Jimmy and more Johns than a hooker could service on a busy Saturday night. It was great fodder for those who did not like the Irish ("Let's call it a *Paddy* wagon!") but it was also trite and boring—something the Irish have never been accused of.

The first dramatic shift over to Irish names happened when the Gaelic League came into being in the 1890s and members started Gaelicizing their names (John became "Seán" and Jane became "Sinéad"). And it became common for Irish revolutionaries after the 1916 Easter Rising to use the Gaelic of, at least, their first names—thus Edward de Valera soon was known to the world as Éamon de Valera.

And like many things in Ireland, the imprint of the Roman Catholic Church is not very far away. Irish saints are part of the legendary make-up of Ireland. Did Patrick really drive the snakes out of Ireland? Who cares! It's great color. (Ironically, St. Patrick was chronically anti-clerical James Joyce's favorite saint. "He was modest and he was sincere," observed Joyce.) Was St. Colmcille really a protector of poets? And what exactly is St. Brigid's Cross? So the Church, which encouraged the traditional use of saint names at baptism, played a part in this transformation, and thus many Irish saint names have been adapted by the young Irish for their children.

The Irish are proud of their saints, and one place they show that national pride is with the national airline, Aer Lingus. Every Aer Lingus plane is named after an Irish saint. On one side of the nose of the plane is the saint's name in English; on the other side it is spelled in Irish.

At look at just some of the saint names on Aer Lingus jets is an education in itself. The most prominent names fly in the long haul fleet, which usually means across the North Atlantic. Here's a sampling, English first/Irish second:

This Aer Lingus plane is named St. Mobhi.

Aoife/Aoife	Maeve/Meadhbh
Columba/Colmcille	Mella/Mella
Conleth/Conlaed	Munchin/Maincín
Davnet/Damhnait	Patrick/Padraig
Fergus/Feargus	Ronan/Ronán
Keeva/Caoimhe	Rowan/Rowan
Laurence O'Toole/Lorcán Tuathail	

The rest of the fleet, servicing mostly European destinations, also has some of the most popular of Irish names:

Aidan/Aodhan	Flannan/Flannan
Aideen/Etaoin	Ibar/Ibhar
Albert/Ailbhe	Ida/Íte
Brendan/Breandan	Jarlath/Iarlaithe mac Loga
Brigid/Brighid	Kealin/Caoilfhionn
Caimin/Caimin	Kevin/Caoimhe
Canice/Cainneach	Kieran/Ciaran
Ciara/Ciara	Kilian/Cillian
Colman/Colman	Macartan/Macárthain

Conleth/Connlaodh	Malachy/Maolmhaodhóg
Davnet/Dymphna	Mel/Mel
Declan/Deaglan	Mobhi/Mobhi
Dervilla/Dearbhile	Moling/Moling
Emer/Eimear	Munchin/Maincín
Enda/Eanna	Nathy/Nathi
Eugene/Eoghan	Oliver Plunkett/Oilibhéar Pluincéid
Eunan/Eunan	Pappin/Paipan
Fachtna/Fachtna	Schira/Scire
Fergal/Fearghal	Senan/Seanan
Fidelma/Fiedeilme	Ultan/Ultan

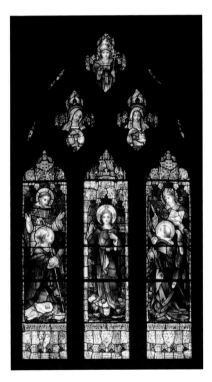

Saint Saviour's Church in Dublin

And just as saint names have influenced this new trend, so have traditional names out of Ireland's historical and mythological past. Here's a list of popular Irish names that you'll be familiar with, this time Irish name first, then the English translation (if any):

Girls	Boys
Áine/Anne	Cathal/Charles
Aisling	Cormac
Caitlín/Catherine or Kathleen	Darragh
Clár/Clare	Diarmuid/Dermot or Jeremiah
Clodagh	Dónal/Donald
Eibhlin/Evelyn	Éamon/Edward
Eimhear/Eimear	Liam/William
Gráinne/Grace	Micheál/Michael (pronounced Me-haul)
Máire/Mary	Néall/Niall
Mairéad/Margaret	Óisín
Niamh/Neeve	Peadar/Peter
Orfhlaith/Orla, Orlagh	Pól/Paul
Róisín/Rosheen	Risteard/Richard
Saoirse (Irish word for "freedom")	Roibeárd/Robert
Sinéad/Jane	Ruairí/Rory or Roger
Siobhán/Joan	Seán/John (MANY spelling variations)
Sorcha or Sive/Sarah	Seosamh/Joseph
Teamhair/Tara	Tadhg/Timothy
	Tomás/Thomas

22

IRELAND'S AMAZING JEWS

It is often said that the Irish are one of the ten lost tribes of Israel. True or not, Ireland has become a landing spot for a tiny but influential population of Jews who have had a giant impact on the nation's culture and politics.

It is believed that the first Jews, probably merchants, hit the Irish shores in 1079. In 1871 the Jewish population of Ireland was only 258. But by 1904—because of pogroms on the continent—it had grown to 4,000, peaking at 5,500 just after World War II. According to the 2011 Irish Census there are only 1,984 Jews presently living in Ireland.

Jews and the Fight for Irish Freedom

The mere establishment of the Irish State may have been impossible without Jewish assistance. Michael Collins depended on his friend, **Michael Noyek** (sometimes spelled "Noyk"), in many areas. Noyek was Collins's real estate man, renting secret offices all over Dublin for the "Big Fellow's" various government portfolios. He also represented *Sinn Féin* rebels in British courts. And he lent his financial expertise when Collins was appointed the nation's first minister for finance, authorized with trying to raise a national loan to finance the new state. Noyek died in 1966 and was given a full military funeral.

Robert Briscoe will always be famous for becoming the first Jewish lord mayor of Dublin in 1956 (he was eventually followed by his son, Ben, in that office). During the War of Independence Briscoe procured guns for Michael Collins on his various business trips to Germany and was responsible for the delivery of weapons to IRA battalions around the country. He later became one of the foremost Zionists in Ireland before Israel was established. He went on to serve thirty-eight years in *Dáil Éireann*.

Yitzhak "Isaac" HaLevi Herzog

At the time of the War of Independence the Chief Rabbi of Ireland was **Yitzhak "Isaac" HaLevi Herzog.** He was a strong supporter of the IRA and the quest for Irish independence. He became a fluent speaker of Irish and was known as "the *Sinn Féin* rabbi." "My father," remembered his son Chaim, "was an open partisan of the Irish cause. When Irish prisoners went on a hunger strike, he pleaded with them to cease endangering their lives. In many circles in Ireland, our family name is still associated with those who fought for liberty." Rabbi Herzog lived in Dublin's "Little Jerusalem," on Bloomfield Avenue (just off the South Circular Road) in the Portobello section of Dublin. A plaque was unveiled at this residence by his son, **Chaim Herzog,** who would go on to become the sixth president of Israel.

One of the tragic figures of Irish history, who ended up dying for Ireland, wasn't an Irishman at all. His name was Abraham Weeks (sometimes known as "Wix"), a London Jew who, trying to avoid conscription in World War I, found himself in Dublin just before the Easter Rising. A fervent socialist, he ended up with James Connolly at Liberty Hall on Easter Monday and soon found himself in the General Post Office as the revolution commenced. At the end of Easter week, when the GPO was in flames, he made his escape with other rebels to Moore Street, just across the way from the GPO. Weeks was mortally wounded and as far as anyone knows, became the first Jew to die in the fight for Irish independence.

"Pulling a Briscoe" — Jewish Lord Mayors

Although **Robert Briscoe** might be Ireland's most famous Jewish lord mayor, he is not the first or only Jewish lord mayor in Irish history. Briscoe was a distant second (by only 401 years) behind **William Annyas,** who was elected lord mayor of Youghal, County Cork, in 1555.

In fact, Briscoe wasn't even the first Jewish lord mayor of Dublin. That honor went to **Lewis Wormser Harris,** who was elected lord mayor in 1876, but died before he could take office.

Ben Briscoe, Robert's son, would be Dublin's lord mayor in 1988–89.

Otto Jaffe was a native of Germany who became a naturalized British citizen, settling in Belfast. A member of the Unionist Party, he was twice elected lord mayor of Belfast in 1899 and 1904.

And **Gerald Goldberg**, whose Lithuanian parents were waylaid in Ireland on their way to America, became the lord mayor of Cork City in 1977.

Anti-Semitism in Ireland

Ireland, compared to other countries, does not have a virulent history of anti-Semitism. "I was fortunate in living in a country," wrote Robert Briscoe in his autobiography, *For the Life of Me,* "where we Jews were subject to no persecution and very little prejudice, far less even than in the United States of America. The terrible pressures which forced European Jews into compact, self-defensive communities were totally absent in Ireland."

"Ireland," said Chaim Herzog in his autobiography, *Living History,* "had no history of anti-Semitism, and while I did not feel outcast, I did feel different. I was always aware that somewhere in the background I was being judged by different standards. When a Jew was arrested for a crime, the entire Jewish community shuddered, because it was expected that all Jews would be thought guilty of that crime. There was an absence of psychological equality."

President Herzog went on to add: "Yet, on many occasions some stones were thrown at us by young urchins, who believed that this was the best way to settle the account with the Jewish people for allegedly crucifying Christ."

Probably the most rabid case of Irish anti-Semitism happened in Limerick City in 1904 (it was, however, preceded by other anti-Semite activities in Limerick in the late nineteenth century). Known as the "Limerick Boycott," or the "Limerick

Chaim Herzog

Pogrom" to Jews, it was initiated by a priest named John Creagh to ostracize Jewish businesses in the city. He claimed the Jews had come to Limerick "to fasten themselves on us like leeches and to draw our blood." Creagh's words soon incited attacks on the small Jewish community. (The Redemptionist Order soon tired of Father Creagh and shipped him to far-away Australia.) Several Jewish families left Limerick—although some later returned—including the family of Gerald Goldberg, the future lord mayor of Cork.

From Griffith, to Gogarty, to Joyce—with an Assist from Sam Beckett

Strangely enough, the history of Irish anti-Semitism is often seen through the prism of four famous Irish Christians—Arthur Griffith, Oliver St. John Gogarty, James Joyce, and Samuel Beckett. The four—all could be described as genuine egalitarians—saw the Jewish experience through different insights. Griffith and Gogarty were known to bait the Jews in their writings, while Joyce and Beckett were known to defend Jews from their attacks.

Ireland is a small country, and Dublin is a smaller town. Back in 1904 everybody seemed to know *everyone*. (How's this for an unlikely coupling? The austere Pádraig Pearse was the Irish teacher of the hedonist-in-training James Joyce. True.) Griffith and Gogarty were friends. Gogarty and Joyce were roommates at the old Martello Tower out in Sandycove, and Griffith was known to visit them there. So Gogarty, Griffith, and Joyce had more than a casual relationship. Although Beckett would not be born until 1906, he became secretary to Joyce in Paris and would have been aware of Gogarty as one of the town's foremost physicians, writers, and wits.

The Limerick Boycott was encouraged, strangely enough, by one of the great democrats in Irish history, Arthur Griffith. Griffith, who in 1922 would help birth the new Irish nation with Michael Collins, took Father Creagh's side in his newspaper, the *United Irishman*. He was a fierce proponent of two of Creagh's attacks—blaming the Jews for usury and being Freemasons, the secret anti-Catholic organization. Although there is no trace of anti-Semitism later in his life, his anti-Semitism is an ugly blot on Griffith's character. (Ironically, Griffith would become a close friend of famed Jewish IRA barrister Michael Noyek, who was also his solicitor.) It should be pointed out that Michael Davitt, the founder of the Land League, attacked those responsible for the riots in the *Freeman's Journal*. Joe Briscoe, another of Robert Briscoe's sons, called the Limerick Boycott "an aberration in an otherwise almost perfect history of Ireland its treatment of the Jews."

The relationship between Gogarty and Joyce was, to say the least, prickly. Friends and roommates at one point, they became estranged. Gogarty went on to become the foremost ear, nose, and throat doctor in Ireland, a writer and poet of distinction, and close friend to the likes of Griffith, Collins, and W.B. Yeats. Conversely, Joyce left Ireland, eventually settling in Paris, and produced the most famous novel of the twentieth century—*Ulysses*. The "Stately, plump Buck Mulligan" of the opening line is, of course, Gogarty, medical student. To put it mildly, after the publication of *Ulysses*, their relationship was not benevolent.

(When I was in college one of my professors, Edward C. McAleer, who knew Gogarty and was a fellow faculty member with him somewhere down in Virginia around 1950, told a story in class about how he and Gogarty were walking along and McAleer innocently asked him, "Why did you call Joyce 'Kinch, the knifeblade' in *Ulysses*?" Gogarty exploded at him: "None of your fucking business!")

In 1935 Gogarty published *As I Was Going Down Sackville Street*, a reminiscence of the Dublin he knew so intimately. He was sued for libel by Harry Sinclair, a Dublin Jewish art dealer, charging that Gogarty had attacked his deceased twin brother, William, and also his grandfather who had been convicted, as Gogarty wrote, for "entic[ing] little girls into his office." Gogarty claimed the characters were composites and had nothing to do with the Sinclairs.

Enter Samuel Beckett, then an unknown, struggling novelist, who had just returned to Dublin after being Joyce's amanuensis in Paris. He claimed for the prosecution that he had recognized the Sinclairs from Gogarty's description and was denounced by Gogarty's counsel as a "bawd and blasphemer." (Beckett's work, *Horoscope*, also came under the microscope.) Beckett failed to note on the stand that not only had he worked for Gogarty's erstwhile friend, Joyce, but was also in love with Peggy Sinclair, Harry Sinclair's niece, and his cousin. He also failed to mention that Harry Sinclair had asked him to purchase the book. Gogarty lost the case and was forced to pay a £900 fine and court costs. "The Jew sold his stinking past," said Gogarty, "dug up a skeleton!" Soon thereafter Gogarty self-exiled himself— à la Joyce—to New York City for the rest of his life.

All this brings us to Joyce and Leopold Bloom, the protagonist of *Ulysses*, and one of the richest characters in literature. Bloom was supposedly born in the Jewish ghetto on Clanbassil Street. (The plaque on the house, just south of the South Circular Road, reads: "Here, in Joyce's imagination was born in May 1866 Leopold Bloom—Citizen, Husband, Father, Wanderer, Reincarnation of Ulysses." Although Bloom is only half Jewish and has become a Roman Catholic, he is still considered Jewish by his Dublin acquaintances. *Ulysses* takes place on June 16, 1904, only six months after the Limerick Boycott. Reading Griffith's *United Irishman*, Joyce must have been well aware of the controversy before he left Ireland in October 1904. Joyce incorporates several snide anti-Semitic remarks into his text as Mister Bloom travels around Dublin City that day.

In Chapter 2: Nestor, Mister Deasy says: "Ireland, they say, has the honour of being the only country which never persecuted the jews. Do you know that? No. And do you know why? . . . Because she never let them in."

In Chapter 12: Cyclops, Mister Bloom says: "Your God was a jew. Christ was a jew like me." Whereas the citizen retorts: "By Jesus, says he, I'll brain that bloody jewman for using the holy name. By Jesus, I'll crucify him so I will."

One often wonders how the life and works of both Griffith and Gogarty—and his animosity towards them—impacted Joyce's view of the Irish Jew. Let the scholars debate!

The Irish Jewish Museum

The Irish Jewish Museum is located on Walworth Street in the Portobello section of Dublin, very near the Grand Canal. It was opened by President Herzog of Israel in 1985 and contains, on the first floor, many items dealing with Jewish life in Ireland. On the second floor there is a synagogue. Ironically, the Museum is located next to the building where Irish actors Barry Fitzgerald and Arthur Shields were born. Both Fitzgerald and Shields made a living in Hollywood playing Catholic priests, although both were Church of Ireland Protestants. Walworth Street represents the best of the Orange and Green and the Star of David!

Irish Jewish Museum in Dublin

The Museum is a short walk to the home that Rabbi Herzog used when he was chief rabbi of Ireland. A plaque on that building on Bloomfield Avenue marks the spot. For more information about the Jewish Museum and the history of the Jews of Ireland check out: www.JewishIreland.org.

Other Prominent Irish Jews

Daniel Day-Lewis—London-born Irish actor (*My Left Foot, Lincoln*) whose mother was Jewish.

Gustav Wilhelm Wolff—The "Wolff" in Harland & Wolff, Belfast shipbuilders of the *Titanic*. He was born in Germany, but immigrated to Britain and then Belfast. Also served as an MP for the Unionist Party for eighteen years.

Alan Shatter—Fine Gael TD who was formerly the minister for justice and equality and minister for defence. Born in Dublin, he was the only Jewish member of *Dáil Éireann*.

Henry Barron—Irish supreme court justice, the first Jew to serve on the court. He granted the Republic's first divorce in 1997.

Estella Solomons—artist and *Cumann na mBan* member. For more, see Chapter 7: Ferocious Fenian Women.

23

THE IRISH WILL ALWAYS
HAVE PARIS

A s Rick (Humphrey Bogart) famously said to Ilsa (Ingrid Bergman) in *Casablanca,* "We'll always have Paris." And the Irish couldn't agree more.

When James Joyce wrote in *Portrait of the Artist as a Young Man* that he must find "silence, exile and cunning" he was probably thinking of Paris, always a refuge to the Irish who sought self-exile like Joyce did, or were forced by the British to leave Ireland because of their political activities.

When most people think of the Irish in exile, the first place that pops to mind is America, particularly New York City. After the failed rising of 1867 many rebels settled in New York, including John Devoy and Jeremiah O'Donovan Rossa. They would later be joined by Tom Clarke after his release from prison in the late 1890s for his involvement in the Invincibles' English bombing campaign. Clarke, who became an American citizen (naturalized in Brooklyn), would return to Dublin to plan the Easter Rising and would be later executed for his trouble.

But while New York may have its honor roll of celebrated Fenians, it should be remembered that Paris has been a happy landing place for Irish rebels since the time of Wolfe Tone. In fact, the City of Light has been a safe haven for both Irish political and cultural refugees.

Welcome United Irishmen

Theobald Wolfe Tone, in anticipation of the Rising of 1798, arrived in Paris in 1796 with the task of pleading for French support for the future insurrection. While there he fell under the influence of the famous American troublemaker, Thomas Paine: "I have lately been introduced to the famous Thomas Paine," wrote Wolfe Tone in his memoirs, "and like him very well. He is vain beyond all belief, but he has reason to be vain, and for my part I forgive him." At this same time Wolfe Tone's comrade, Lord Edward Fitzgerald, was the roommate of Paine in Paris. Both Wolfe Tone and Fitzgerald would return to Ireland to lead the disastrous 1798 Rising and would pay with their lives for their revolutionary acts. Likewise, the Sheares Brothers, Henry and John, caught the revolutionary bug during the French Revolution in Paris. Like Wolfe Tone and Lord Edward, they would be executed for their part in the 1798 insurrection. Robert Emmet fled Dublin after 1798 and lived in Paris while he planned his 1803 revolt. He sought the support of Napoleon but events did not coalesce in Emmet's favor, and no French help was forthcoming.

1848 and 1867

James Stephens—the revolutionary, not the writer—moved to Paris after the 1848 uprising. He eventually returned to Ireland and became a persistent revolutionary gadfly right under the nose of the British. He was a one of the founders of the Irish Republican Brotherhood (IRB) and involved in the planning of the 1867 Rising. When the British discovered the plans for the revolt Stephens was arrested and imprisoned. He escaped and again returned to Paris. He died in 1901.

John O'Mahony was another refugee from the 1848 revolt. He lived in Paris for a time until moving to New York where he founded the IRB in 1859.

John O'Leary, after his conviction for "treason felony" in 1865, served time in British prisons until he arrived in Paris in 1871. He remained there until 1885 when he returned to Dublin. He would have great influence over W.B. Yeats, Maud Gonne, and others and would be remembered by Yeats in "September 1913": *"Romantic Ireland's dead and gone/it's with O'Leary in the grave."*

Although **John Mitchel** spent most of his time in exile in America, he did live in Paris for a time while he did work for the Fenians.

It should be noted that while Mitchel, O'Mahony, Stephens, and O'Leary (and even Wolfe Tone and Emmet, to a lesser extent) are known for their revolutionary exploits, all four of them made their living, at one time or another, as journalists, setting the stage for twentieth century Irish writers who would have a great revolutionary effect—this time literary—on the world.

Maud Gonne's Paris

Perhaps the one Irish artist and revolutionary with the most permanent attachment to Paris, and France, was Maud Gonne. She was educated there after the death of her mother, and it was there that she met her first common-law husband, Lucien Millevoye. It was with Millevoye that Gonne had two children, including her precocious daughter, Iseult. In 1903 she married John (Seán) MacBride and the following year their son, Seán, was born. When her marriage to MacBride disintegrated, Gonne remained in Paris with her children until MacBride was executed by the British in 1916, and only then did she return to Ireland on a permanent basis.

Maud Gonne in 1900.

James Joyce and His Circle

As if signaling that the time was ripe, James Joyce arrived to Paris just after the conclusion of World War I. His arrival was followed by the "Lost Generation" of writers such as Hemingway, Eliot, and Fitzgerald. Actually, this was Joyce's second trip to Paris. In 1901 he arrived ostensibly to study medicine, but returned to Dublin when his mother fell ill. Joyce's exile in Europe was mostly in Trieste and Zurich, and his arrival in Paris was heralded in literary circles.

Joyce found Paris to his liking and he lived there for twenty years until he fled to Zurich with the Nazi blitzkrieg of 1940. During his time there, *Ulysses* was published on February 2, 1922 — his "lucky," he thought, fortieth birthday. Joyce was followed to Paris by many Irish friends, including Thomas McGreevy and Padraic Colum. Colum introduced him to James Stephens, author of *The Crock of Gold,* and they became fast friends.

Joyce was very superstitious, particularly about numbers, reports Colum in the book he wrote with his wife, Mary, *Our Friend James Joyce.* Joyce probably took to Stephens because not only were both Dubliners and writers, but they shared the exact same birthday — February 2, 1882. Colum recalls once that at a dinner party for eleven, Stephens called and said he would be dropping by with a friend, bringing the number to an unlucky thirteen! Joyce immediately sought out another guest to bring the number to a salubrious fourteen. Colum also recalls Joyce running into actress Marlene Dietrich at a restaurant: "I saw you," Joyce said to the star, as if he were speaking of some event far back in history, "in L'Ange blue [The Blue Angel]." "Then, monsieur," Miss Dietrich replied, "you saw the best of me."

Samuel Beckett Reaches Mr. Joyce at Ségur 95-20

And it was during his Paris sojourn that the bulk of the work on *Finnegans Wake* was done. Since Joyce's blindness made writing a difficult task, he was soon joined by a Dublin amanuensis by the name of Samuel Beckett, who was introduced to Joyce by mutual friend Thomas McGreevy. Although both Joyce and Beckett were Dubliners and world-class writers, they came from different backgrounds. Joyce was Catholic and at times lived in near poverty, whereas Beckett was from the well-manicured Protestant suburb of Foxrock and never really wanted in the same way financially.

Colum recollects in his book how Joyce, because of his vision problems, depended heavily on his friends. Noel Riley Fitch recalls in her book, *Sylvia Beach and the Lost Generation*, how Joyce would beckon and how Beckett would respond immediately: "Beckett reached for her phone and gave the operator the number: Ségur 95-20. *Ségur quatre-vingt-quinze-vingt,* he spoke the words with a poetic rhythm that he would remember vividly for more than five decades. Joyce wanted a companion for his evening walk, and Beckett hurried to meet him, honored by the demand, which it was a privilege to fulfill."

Joyce and Beckett would be close, but their relationship would have its stormy moments, most famously rocked by the unrequited romantic interest Joyce's mentally disturbed daughter, Lucia, took in Beckett. Joyce and Beckett, however, would reconcile before the start of the war.

At the beginning of the war, Beckett declared that he preferred "France at war to Ireland at peace." After the Nazi invasion he joined the Resistance and barely avoided capture by the Gestapo before fleeing Paris for the French countryside. With the liberation of France he went home to Dublin and soon returned to France as a member of the Irish Red Cross. In 1953 *Waiting for Godot* was performed and a literary giant was born. He would continue to write in French, and France would remain his home for the rest of his life.

Brendan Behan Tracks Down Sam Beckett

As Joyce helped Beckett, Beckett would extend a hand to another Irish expatriate by the name of Brendan Behan. As much as the Dublin backgrounds of Joyce and Beckett differed, the backgrounds of Behan and Beckett were from different solar systems.

Behan was born into the slums of Northside Dublin—although it should be pointed out that the tenement he lived in was owned by his granny—and his whole family were staunch Republicans. His uncle Peadar Kearney wrote the Irish national anthem, "*Amhrán na bhFiann*" ("The Soldier's Song"). His father took part in the burning of the Customs House in Dublin in 1921 and his mother was a friend of Michael Collins, who she affectionately referred to as her "laughing boy."

Behan had served time in both British and Irish prisons—the genesis for his *Borstal Boy*—for his IRA activities, and because of his problems with drink and lack of writing production he decided to go to Paris for a change of scenery. His first mission there? To track down fellow Dublin writer Samuel Beckett, who was beginning to make a name for himself.

Behan read a piece on Beckett in *Merlin* magazine by American Richard Seaver. Of course he figured the best way to meet

Samuel Beckett in 1977.

Beckett was by accosting the unassuming Seaver. In one of the great descriptions of the color, profanity, and genius of Behan's speech, Seaver recalls in his memoir, *The Tender Hour of Twilight,* the first thing Behan said to him: "I missed Joyce," Behan began. "I hated that fucking Yeats. Flann O'Brien leaves me cold. He's so fucking *Irish.* The same goes for John Millington Synge, who stuck his fucking ear to the fucking wall to overhear how the peasants really talk, then put it into his fucking plays as though he'd made it up himself! Damned thief! Anyway, from what you wrote about Beckett, he sounds like the real thing. So tell me how to find him." Behan—a "cute 'hoor" as they like to say in Dublin—said of Beckett: "He'll receive me the same way Joyce received him."

A wary Seaver—who would be instrumental with Barney Rosset in bringing Beckett's work to American readers—tried to put Behan off, but Brendan was persistent. Seaver left messages to warn Beckett, but the relentless Behan tracked him down anyway—at six o'clock in the morning! He occupied Beckett for three hours until Beckett had to leave for a rehearsal of *Waiting for Godot.*

"Samuel Beckett," wrote Ulick O'Connor in his Behan biography *Brendan*, "also met him at this time and was pleasant to him in a slightly sad, sardonic Dublin accent. Beckett, like Joyce, was always pleased to meet Dubliners in exile . . ."

Beckett himself confided to Seaver: "Poor lad, at the rate he's drinking, he won't last another decade."

Beckett was right. Behan returned to Dublin, became internationally famous for *Borstal Boy, The Quare Fellow,* and *The Hostage.* Celebrity would kill him in a decade.

24
TITANIC TO VIAGRA: MADE IN IRELAND

Ireland's greatest export has always been her people, but she is also known for many of her manufactured products. These range from crystals to linens to alcoholic beverages, such as Guinness and a wide range of Irish whiskeys.

But probably Ireland's most famous product ended in disaster and has become a legend that never ceases to amaze even one hundred years after her death. That would be the RMS *Titanic*.

The Legend of *Titanic*

The building of *Titanic* in Belfast is really the story of the rivalry between the Cunard and White Star lines. Early in the twentieth century, Cunard ruled the North Atlantic with her dual greyhound steamships named *Mauretania* and *Lusitania*. As immigration from the continent and Ireland increased, both Cunard and White Star discovered how grand first class was and how profitable steerage could be because of America's new immigrants. So, to compete with Cunard, White Star decided to build three big liners of its own—*Olympic, Titanic,* and *Britannic.* These ships were not as fast as Cunard's flying greyhounds, but were more luxurious, built for comfort not speed, easily five knots slower than the Cunarders.

Olympic was launched in 1911 with Captain Edward Smith as her master. Right behind *Olympic* on the ways at Harland & Wolff was *Titanic*. By April 1912 she was on her maiden voyage with Captain Smith at the helm. She left Southampton, advanced to Cherbourg in France, and her last port-of-call was Queenstown (now Cobh) in County Cork. There she took on 113 Irish passengers for her steerage compartment. As she left Cork behind, she didn't know it was the last piece of real estate she would ever see. *Titanic* hit an iceberg near midnight on April 14, 1912, and sunk in the early morning hours of April 15—and a legend was born.

The legend of *Titanic* was famously revived by Walter Lord's gripping history, *A Night to Remember*, published in 1955. It was followed three years later by a British motion picture of the same name starring Kenneth More as Second Officer Charles Lightoller. The film, which follows Lord's book faithfully, still holds up after fifty years as the most definitive and accurate story of the sinking.

The Titanic *under construction in Belfast, 1911–1912.*

The more popular, "sexy" version of *Titanic* was captured in the 1997 James Cameron film starring Leonard DiCaprio and Kate Winslet. (Both movies were preceded in 1953 by 20th Century Fox's *Titanic*, starring Barbara Stanwyck and Clifton Webb.)

Oddly enough, the bad luck of *Titanic* seemed also to haunt her sister ships. *Olympic*, only a year older, went on to a full career before being scrapped in 1935. She was, however, unlucky, becoming involved in three major collisions during her career. *Britannic* soon followed *Titanic* off the ways. There was a rumor— although this has been disputed—that originally White Star planned to call the third sister ship *Gigantic*, but decided not to tempt fate again and renamed her *Britannic*. But *Britannic* shared the unlucky streak of her sisters and while serving as a hospital ship during World War I she hit a mine in the Aegean Sea in 1916 and sunk. (One of the remarkable characters of history was stewardess/nurse Violet Jessop, who was on the *Olympic* when it collided with a British cruiser in 1911, and survived *both* the sinkings of *Titanic* and *Britannic*.)

"3909-04."

To many Catholics, even today, *Titanic* is still thought of as a bigoted Protestant product of Belfast. Why? Well, due to prejudice few Catholics actually worked at Harland & Wolff, and those who did were often harassed and worried about hammers being dropped on their heads.

The legend among Catholics that will not die says that Harland & Wolff assigned *Titanic* the ship number "3909-04." Many Catholics still maintain that if you print the number on a piece of paper and hold it up to a mirror you'll receive a special message from the Protestant builders of *Titanic*—NO POPE! This canard has been thoroughly disputed, but the Irish are well aware of the old adage: if the facts get in the way of the legend, print the legend!

Titanic Belfast

The legend of *Titanic* has turned the ship's birthplace into a tourist attraction. Titanic Belfast is one of the most popular tourist attractions in all of Ireland. Located on Queen's Island on the former location where *Titanic* and her sisters were built, it is dedicated to the story and legend of the doomed liner, where visitors can absorb the *Titanic* experience from keel to tomb. Opened in 2012, it drew over 800,000 spectators. Besides tours and information, according to its website, it is an excellent place to hold one's wedding reception—if you feel like tempting fate, I suppose.

Viagra—Up the Irish!

Throughout the world most men and—I guess—women don't know what a debt of gratitude they owe to Ringaskiddy, County Cork. For it is in Ringaskiddy, since the late 1990s, that Pfizer, the giant pharmaceutical company, has manufactured the erection dysfunction drug, Viagra. Known fondly by the locals as the "Pfizer Riser" or the "Cork Elixir & Fixer," the legend is that it is the home of the happiest men in Ireland, no matter what their age. Some think that it may have something to do with the Cork water. It is famously remembered in parts of Cork that heroic Irish revolutionary Michael Collins was born when his father was in his seventy-eighth year.

And as the old saying goes, "What's good enough for Mick Collins is good enough for me!"

Belfast Linen—The Stubborn Industry

In "The Ballad of William Bloat" by Raymond Calvert, the title character lived on Shankill Road, the center of militant Protestantism. So sang the Clancy Brothers and Tommy Makem in the 1960s. They were singing about a man who is sick of his wife, cuts her throat, and in remorse for what he has done, decides to hang himself. Unfortunately for him, the wife survives while he succeeds in his death quest: *"For the razor blade was German-made/But the rope was Belfast linen."*

In this commercial for the power of Belfast linen one might notice several things right away, namely that it was a Protestant industry (the Shankill Road in Belfast is Protestant territory) and that the sturdy Protestant strain endures, even in their linen.

Linen is the fabric made from the cultivated flax plant, and its history in Ireland goes as far back as the sixteenth century. By the 1700s it accounted for about half of Ireland's total exports. Always competing against England's wool industry, the American Civil War proved a boom for Ireland's linen industry because of the shortage of cotton coming out of the Confederate states due to the Union naval blockade. By the time of the First World War Belfast was known worldwide as "Linenopolis." World War II saw the linen industry at its apex, but following the war the industry suffered greatly as it approached extinction. Today, although in a tremendously reduced state from its heyday, the industry still strives for quality, and it is this quality that makes Irish linen the treasured product it remains to this day.

Irish Crystal—A Story of Survival

The term "Waterford Crystal" summons up visions of an ancient Irish industry, hundreds of years in the making. In a way you would be right—but you'd also be wrong. Although the history of crystal manufacturing in Ireland goes back as far as 1771, the crystal industry, like Ireland herself, has had its ups and downs. In the late

The Waterford crystal factory in Waterford, County Waterford, Ireland.

eighteenth century, crystal manufacturing had taken hold in both Counties Tyrone and Waterford. By 1818 there was also enterprise in Cork. But the Great Famine of the 1840s decimated the industry as many skilled craftsmen disappeared.

For one hundred years the crystal industry went dormant in Ireland. It was not until after World War II that the industry revived when, in 1947, Czech immigrant Charles Bacik opened a factory in Waterford and imported skilled workers from the continent. Waterford Crystal quickly became synonymous worldwide with quality cut glass.

The industry continues to survive despite many hardships, including closings and labor disputes. Today crystal is made in many parts of Ireland. All the locations have sprung up since the end of World War II making crystal "a new old Irish industry." Besides Waterford, crystal factories can be found in Galway, Belfast, Cork, Dublin, and Tipperary. Sadly, Tyrone Crystal ceased operations in 2010.

Spirited Spirits

While linen and crystal have fought for survival in Ireland, the alcoholic beverage industry—particularly Guinness and Irish whiskey—have flourished. In fact, according to the Distilled Spirits Council, Irish whiskey sales in the United States have increased 485 percent since 2002.

Today Irish whiskey is made at three primary locations in Ireland: Bushmills Distillery in County Antrim, Cooley Distillery in County Louth, and Midleton Distillery in County Cork.

Bushmills claims to be the "World's Oldest Whiskey Distillery" because its license for distilling dates to 1608. Its products include Bushmills, Black Bush, and 16-Year-Old Bushmills single malt. It is now part of Diageo, the spirits conglomerate, owner of Guinness, Bailey's, and Johnnie Walker Scotch whisky.

The Cooley Distillery in Dundalk is the Johnny-come-lately of Irish distillers having only been formed in the late 1980s. Its products include the John Lock and Tyrconnell brands as well as Connemara, a pure pot still and Ireland's only peated single malt whiskey. Cooley also produces supermarket brand whiskeys. The brands are matured in Kilbeggan in County Westmeath, where there is also a museum opened to the public. It was purchased in 2011 by Beam, Inc.

The Midleton Distillery, owned by the Irish Distillers Group, produces probably the three most famous brands of Irish whiskey—Jameson, Paddy, and Powers. The old Jameson factory on Bow Street in Dublin continues to conduct tours of the old plant.

A growing industry, new Irish whiskey distilleries are planned for Carlow, Kerry, Derry, and the famed Liberties in Dublin's inner city.

Guinness's "Black Beer"

Since John Wayne famously asked for a "Black Beer" in *The Quiet Man,* Ireland and the world have had a romance with stout. Brewed since 1759—as the bottle proclaims—at St. James's Gate, Dublin, Guinness is as an integral part of Dublin as O'Connell Street, the GPO, or Trinity College. It is available in over 120 countries

The Guinness Brewery in Dublin.

worldwide and it would be hard not to find it on any continent, except for Antarctica. Its annual sales total 850 million liters—almost two billion U.S. pints. And the tour at the Guinness Storehouse and a pint afterwards at the Gravity Bar—with perhaps the best panoramic view of Dublin—is one of Ireland's leading tourist attractions.

Sláinte!

25

WHAT THE HELL IS BLACK PUDDING? ADVENTURES IN IRISH CUISINE

T he joke among the Irish when I was a kid was that the Americans had Julia Child and *Mastering the Art of French Cooking* while the Irish had to depend on *The Joy of Boiling* as their cookbook guide. You know, boil it for a couple of hours, then another fifteen minutes—to be sure, to be sure.

Well things have changed over the years. Today Ireland boasts some of the best food and seafood in the world, and their chefs have been trained at some of the finest culinary institutes on the continent. From Belfast to Dublin to Dingle, Ireland is sprinkled with some of the finest restaurants in the world.

One only has to look at the local PBS station to see how the Irish have embraced the culinary arts. PBS cooking shows include *Kevin Dundon's Modern Irish Food, Clodagh's (McKenna) Irish Food Trails,* and *Neven Maguire: Home Chef.* But as much as the Irish have embraced twenty-first century cooking innovations, they still have a place in their heart for some of the old-time favorites.

The Fry-Up

It's hard to come into a house in Ireland, even to this day, without being offered a "fry-up" and a cup of good sweet tea. Of course, any fry has to contain all the ingredients: fried egg, sausage, black pudding and white pudding (often called "Drisheen"), Irish bacon ("rashers"), fried tomato, and a good slab of bread inundated with rich yellow Irish butter. (You're also liable to get a few fried mushrooms and some baked beans.) It's always a delight to watch Americans bite into their first sampling of black and white pudding. "This is delicious! What is it?" You wait for the swallow then tell: "Blood sausage." The reaction is worth the wait. The

Black and White Pudding Slices

term "blood sausage" makes Americans queasy, although it's very popular throughout Europe, from France to Poland. Actually, black pudding is truly a blood sausage (pork, water, oats, beef blood, barley, onion, salt, dextrose, spices, mustard, monosodium glutamate, spice extractive, sodium nitrite), while white pudding (pork, water, oats, barley, onion, salt, dextrose, spices, sodium nitrite) tends to be spicier and *sans* blood. Irish bacon is also more like Canadian bacon than American bacon, and unlike its Canadian partner, retains most of its fat.

Irish Delicacies

There are many dishes on Irish menus that sound familiar but can be a complete mystery to Americans. Here are a few. (Note that you won't find corned beef and cabbage, a pseudo-Irish American concoction probably derived from the Irish affection for cabbage and bacon.)

Barm Brack—a yeast bread with raisins.

Boxty Bread—a traditional bread made with potato and dough flour. There is even a restaurant in Dublin's Temple Bar named after it, The Boxty House.

The Temple Bar in Dublin.

Colcannon—a dish of mashed potatoes, cabbage, and butter, often served at Halloween.

Crubeens—boiled pig's feet; an ancient Irish fast food from the Irish *cruibini* for "pig's feet." They are fondly remembered in the song "Galway Races":

> *It's there you'll see confectioners with sugarsticks and dainties,*
> *And lozenges and oranges and lemonade and raisins,*
> *And gingerbread and spices to accommodate the ladies,*
> *And a big crubeen for thruppence to be pickin' while you're able.*

The late, great Liam Clancy—called "the greatest balladeer of the twentieth century" by Bob Dylan—once interrupted himself singing "Galway Races" at the mention of the crubeens. "Have the crubeens given away to the old hamburgers as the fast food of the Irish people?" Liam wondered. "I hope not. By God you'd look forward to a feed of crubeens, especially when you took them down on the strand and rolled them around in the sand a couple of times. You'd have the crunch in your teeth for a week after. We'd boil them up and always left a little bit of the hair on them, about half an inch or so, and a bit of dirt in between the two toes for flavoring. Wrapped up in last week's *Munster Express*. By God, the headlines would still be stuck on the back of them. Sure, there was readin' and eatin'."

Dublin Coddle—a casserole of bacon, sausage, and potatoes, which is said to have been a favorite of both Seán O'Casey and Jonathan Swift.

Dublin Lawyer—a luxurious lobster dish with plenty of Irish whiskey and heavy cream.

Haggerty—scalloped potatoes.

Irish Soda Bread—a bread made without yeast, using baking soda and buttermilk as the leavening agent. There is usually a cross-marked across the top of it to help it rise—and keep the faeries out.

Plaice—Ireland is renowned for its seafood—from its Galway oysters to its Dublin Bay prawns (shrimp) to Molly Malone's famous cockles and mussels. And there's also a fish unique to northern European waters that Americans may not be familiar with—plaice. It's like a cross between flounder and sole and it is prepared either fried or baked.

Scones—a cake or quick bread with baking powder used as a leavening agent; often served with tea.

Drinks

Ireland is famous for their drinks—Irish Coffee being the obvious—but here's a few you may not be familiar with:

Black Velvet—a smooth, delicious drink, half Guinness stout and champagne.

Scáiltín—a hot milk punch made with milk, Irish whiskey, honey, and spices.

Shandy—a mixture of beer or ale and lemonade or ginger ale.

26

ANOTHER KIND OF SPIRITS:
GHOSTS, BANSHEES,
LEPRECHAUNS, WAKES, AND
FAERIES,
OR: WAITING FOR THE
THREE KNOCKS AT THE
DOOR

My parents were born in the first decade of the twentieth century. My mother was a proud southside Dubliner who worked the kitchens of the Anglo-Irish in neatly trimmed suburbs like Foxrock. My father was a farmer from Clogher Head, County Louth, the "Wee County" just inside the border of the Republic. One a "Jackeen" and the other a "culchie." Yet, they had one thing in common—an acquaintance, if not a belief, in the occult, something very prevalent in a country full of religion and short on outside influences.

Much of Irish folklore and superstition has been hijacked by Hollywood—there are at least eight Leprechaun movies, not to mention Disney's 1959 film *Darby O'Gill and the Little People,* starring a young Scottish (oh, the humiliation!) actor named Sean Connery, but also featuring the great Irish character actor Jack MacGowran. As for banshee movies, there are also at least ten Hollywood productions with banshee in their titles.

It was not uncommon as a child for my father and his brothers and sisters to sit around and talk about the old country—a rich Irish verbal tradition that has been lost in this age of cell phones and computers. Part of this was the telling of ghost stories. There were stories of disturbed spirits who could only be quelled by intervention by the clergy. Always the youngest cleric in the parish would be sent to pray away the ghost, and soon after the young priest himself would pass away. My father also had stories of digging graves—apparently it was a tradition in farm country to dig a neighbor's grave—and unearthing long dead friends and relatives. (One story that stuck with me was the tale of an old coffin being jarred open and discovering that the corpse—clean shaven in life—now had a long white beard!) My father also said he had seen banshees, keening away, warning of death.

My mother's brush with the supernatural was about the ominous "Three Knocks at the Door"—a sure sign of imminent death. She was taking care of a young boy who was dying in Dublin in the late 1920s. She was alone with the boy, and suddenly there were three knocks at the door. When she answered it, there was no one there. When she returned to the boy, he was dead. It made such an impression on her that she retold the story into her old age.

Of course, this caused a lot of jeering from my worldly father. "Ah," he would say, "you're full of pisterogs!" My father was not an Irish speaker, but Irish words would often color his vocabulary. As an adult I learned that there was a basis for my father's "pisterogs." It derives from the Irish word *piseog*, which means "superstitious." So my father was right about his "pisterogs," even if his Irish pronunciation was off.

So let's put all the Hollywood special effects aside and look at some of the supernatural entities close to the heart of the Irish:

Wakes

The Irish word for wake is *faire*, very close to faery. Today the traditional Irish wake, almost always held in the deceased's home, has gone the way of the American-style funeral parlor. In times past, the purpose of the wake was to ascertain that the dead person was, in fact, dead, and did not waken. It was the job of the mourners to help the departed soul transition to its new life.

My father had a story about a wake that betrayed the seriousness of the mourning. The corpse had a lame leg, and it was decided to tie the leg to the bedpost for appearances' sake. During the rosary, as mourners on bent knees surrounded the departed and recited the rosary, someone took out a pen knife and cut the rope holding the leg down. The leg went straight up into the air and the mourners, rosaries a-flying, trampled each other trying to get out of the room.

Wakes were such a part of the Irish social structure that James Joyce even named his last novel *Finnegans Wake*. Joyce took the title from a popular Dublin music hall song:

> *Mickey Maloney raised his head*
> *When a bottle of whiskey flew at him*
> *It missed and falling on the bed*
> *The liquor scattered over Tim*
> *Tim revives—see how he rises*
> *Timothy rising, from the bed*
> *Sayin': "Whirl your whiskey around like blazes—*
> *Thunderin' Jaysus, do ye think I'm dead?"*

The corpse, a construction laborer by the name of Tim Finnegan, is finally brought back to life when a vat of whiskey is poured over him, giving new meaning to the Irish *uisce beatha*— the "water of life."

Banshee

From the Irish *bean sith* meaning "woman of the faery mounds," the banshee has been a precursor of death to the Irish for centuries. Various legends have her appearing in several forms, mostly as a short, ugly woman, although she can appear as anything she wishes, even a beautiful woman. She is said to often follow certain families and her keening, depending on the part of the country, can range from either being a terrifying wail or as sweet as a song.

Leprechauns

Leprechaun comes from the Irish *leipreachán,* meaning "small." He is a true Irish trickster, capable of cajoling greedy humans who are after his hidden gold. Leprechauns are often described as midget-like and are portrayed as shoemakers with access to crocks of gold. The nineteenth century Donegal poet William Allingham perhaps has done the best job of describing this elusive being in "The Lepracaun: Or the Fairy Shoemaker":

> *I caught him at work one day, myself,*
> *In the castle-ditch, where foxglove grows,—*
> *A wrinkled, wizen'd and bearded Elf,*
> *Spectacles stuck on his pointed nose,*
> *Silver buckles to his hose,*
> *Leather apron-shot in his lap—*

Allingham also describes how the trickster tricks:

> *The rogue was mine, beyond a doubt.*

I stared at him; he stared at me;
"Servant, Sir!" "Humph!" says he,
And pull'd a snuff-box out.
He took a long pinch, look'd better pleased,
The queer little Lepracaun;
Offer'd the box with a whimsical grace, —
Pouf! he flung the dust in my face,
And, while I sneezed,
Was gone!

The legend of the Leprechaun has also been used as a stereotype for the Irish. One just has to look at Thomas Nast's nineteenth-century caricatures of the Irish and the word "leprechaun" is the first thing that jumps to mind.

And the twenty-first century leprechaun has been totally corrupted. Every Saturday afternoon in autumn on national TV, he is a persistent green pugnacious figure—the symbol of Notre Dame's "Fighting Irish." And he is not only a film star in bad movies—he also appears as the spokesman for General Mills cereal "Lucky Charms." In commercials, obviously aimed at kids, he is dressed up in a little green suit and instead of a pot of gold the kids are after his "Lucky Charms." As elusive as ever, just as he did to the poet Allingham, he has been known to fly away after dispensing his bounty to the hungry sugar-starved youngsters.

Faeries

There is probably no myth as entrenched with the Irish as the legend of the faeries. There is no one set definition of a faery. They seem to live an alternate existence to humans, while at the same time assuming many of the physical characteristics of

A depiction of the Irish by nineteenth-century political cartoonist Thomas Nast.

human. They are thought to be the original occupiers of the land and have been driven underground by invaders to Ireland. And they possess many magical powers. One thing is for sure—one should never cross or anger faeries. William Allingham wrote in "The Fairies":

Up the airy mountain
Down the rushy glen,
We daren't go a-hunting,
For fear of little men;

Faeries have been also known to steal babies, replacing them with a "changeling." It was thought that baptism or cold iron could protect the child. Allingham tells such a tale in "The Fairies":

They stole little Bridget
For seven years long;
When she came down again
Her friends were all gone.
They took her lightly back
Between the night and morrow;
They thought she was fast asleep,
But she was dead with sorrow.
They have kept her ever since
Deep within the lake,
On a bed of flag leaves,
Watching till she wake.

Yeats echoed a similar theme in "The Stolen Child":

Come away, O human child!
To the waters and the wild
With a faery, hand in hand,
For the world's more full of weeping than you can understand.

Even in modern times faeries still permeate Irish life. It is still said that someone suffering from dementia in Ireland is "off with the faeries." Then there is the legend of Shannon Airport in County Clare. Back in the 1950s, as new runways for jets were being constructed, workers came across a faery fort—the remaining mound of a prehistoric structure—and refused to remove it. Naturally, so the lore maintains, they moved the runway, not the faery fort. Even in modern, hi-tech Ireland, the faeries get their due.

Ringfort (faery fort) at Cabragh

John "Seán" Ignatius Quinn was one of the wealthiest men in Ireland, with a fortune estimated at €4.7 billion. But greed got the better of him when he decided to move the Aughrim Wedge Tomb in the early 1990s. The megalithic burial site had stood for 4,000 years in County Cavan. But Quinn decided to move it for the expansion of a quarry for Quinn Concrete in 1992. Within two decades there was no need for concrete as the Irish housing market imploded with the execution of the Celtic Tiger. Quinn, heavily involved with the machinations of the Anglo-Irish Bank, went bankrupt and in 2012 found himself in the Irish calaboose. The moral of the story? It seems that Irish entrepreneurs come and go—but faeries last forever.

27

THE CASTRATED CELTIC TIGER:
BEWARE OF FALSE *PROFITS*

Hubris is a terrible thing to behold. It's even worse when it infects the Irish.

Ten years ago every newspaper and financial news network was heaping praise on Ireland's "Celtic Tiger." The Celtic Tiger was the robust name the media gave to the Irish economy which made a *miraculous*—a favorite word for economic pundits—turn-around. Immigration was halted, housing prices went through the roof, and the economy was purring. There was a building boom in progress with members from other EEC countries—particularly Poland—coming to the land of Saints and Scholars to cash in on the exploding economy.

Then in 2010 it stopped exploding and suddenly imploded.

As St. Patrick used the shamrock to explain the Holy Trinity to Ireland's pagans, the shamrock now can be used to explain how the new gombeen men—the banks, the real estate developers, and the politicians—conspired to rape the country's economy for their own interests. And, of course, when the EEC enforced their wonderful austerity plans—after lending $113 billion to Ireland—the banks got off scot-free and the common Irishman and woman were burdened by the greed of the Gombeen Trinity. Today there is a stark reminder of that time—the "Ghost Estates" that populate and disfigure the Irish countryside, relatively new, unoccupied, already crumbling, and serving as an Irish Mount Rushmore to greed.

But memories can be short. In December 2013, *Forbes* magazine announced to the world that Ireland now headed their list of "The Best Countries for Business." Ireland was Numero Uno again! Ireland was back in the business of being in business! *Forbes* knows this because Dublin now serves as the European

Pre-Euro Irish Coin

headquarters for such U.S. social media firms as Google, LinkedIn, Twitter, and Facebook.

It sounds like it is just about time for "Celtic Tiger *Redux*."

But this time around it might be wise for a race of people with a history of national catastrophes to remain suspicious and heed the advice of the Bible: Matthew 7:15: "Beware of the false prophets, who come to you in sheep's clothing, but inwardly are ravenous wolves."

Yes, beware of "false *profits*."

They say that the definition of insanity is doing the same thing over and over again and expecting a different outcome. The Bible covered that one too in Proverbs 26:11: "As a dog returneth to his vomit, so a fool returneth to his folly."

James Connolly and Pádraig Pearse often warned the Irish about fools. One wonders what these two men would think of the Republic—a nation they gave their lives to establish—so blatantly and despicably entrenched in financial hocus-pocus just for the gain of a small minority. If only ghosts could start revolutions. Yes, the revolution will start at the GPO, noon sharp. Let's post it on Facebook and Twitter and wait for the insurrection.

But I don't think so, not this year at least.

PHOTO CREDITS

Chapter 17
http://commons.wikimedia.org/wiki/File:Dublin-Dept-Of-Taoiseach-2012.JPG; copyright 2012 by Bjørn Christian Tørrissen
http://commons.wikimedia.org/wiki/File:%C3%89amon_de_Valera.jpg
http://upload.wikimedia.org/wikipedia/commons/e/e6/Mary_Robinson_World_Economic_Forum_2013_crop.jpg
Chapter 18: Thinkstock
https://www.awesomestories.com/images/user/533ae3cc54.JPG
http://upload.wikimedia.org/wikipedia/commons/7/75/James_Joyce_by_Alex_Ehrenzweig,_1915_cropped.jpg
Chapter 19: Thinkstock
Chapter 20: Thinkstock
http://commons.wikimedia.org/wiki/File:Collier%27s_1921_New_York_(city)_-_Immigration_Station_on_Ellis_Island.jpg
http://commons.wikimedia.org/wiki/File:Liber_Natorum_(examples).jpg
http://www.historyireland.com/20th-century-contemporary-history/the-roll-of-honour-of-1916/
Chapter 21
http://commons.wikimedia.org/wiki/File:Clonard_Statue_St_Finian_2007_08_26.jpg
http://upload.wikimedia.org/wikipedia/commons/2/21/A320_Aer_Lingus_EI-CVB_01.jpg
http://commons.wikimedia.org/wiki/File:Dublin_Saint_Saviour%27s_Dominican_Priory_Church_Outer_South_Aisle_Window_Adoration_of_Jesus_2012_09_26.jpg
Chapter 22
http://commons.wikimedia.org/wiki/File:Jewish_Wedding_at_Waterford_Courthouse_1901.jpg
http://commons.wikimedia.org/wiki/File:Yitzhak_HaLevi_Herzog_1945_portrait.jpg
http://en.wikipedia.org/wiki/File:Presidherzog.jpg
http://commons.wikimedia.org/wiki/File:Jewishmuseum.jpg
Chapter 23
http://commons.wikimedia.org/wiki/File:James_Joyce_with_Sylvia_Beach_at_Shakespeare_%26_Co_Paris_1920.jpg
http://commons.wikimedia.org/wiki/File:Maud_Gonne_cph.3b21750.jpg
http://commons.wikimedia.org/wiki/File:Samuel_Beckett,_Pic,_1.jpg
Chapter 24
http://en.wikipedia.org/wiki/File:RMS_Titanic_ready_for_launch,_1911.jpg
http://en.wikipedia.org/wiki/File:Titanic_under_construction.jpg
http://commons.wikimedia.org/wiki/File:Waterford_Crystal_Building.jpg; copyright 2009 by Ticketautomat
http://commons.wikimedia.org/wiki/File:Guinness_Brewery_Dublin_01_977.PNG
Chapter 25
http://commons.wikimedia.org/wiki/File:Full_irish_breakfast_55.jpg; copyright 2012 by jules
http://commons.wikimedia.org/wiki/File:Irish_black_and_white_pudding_slices.JPG; copyright 2009 by O'Dea
Thinkstock
Chapter 26
http://commons.wikimedia.org/wiki/File:Leprechaun_ill_artlibre_jnl.png
http://commons.wikimedia.org/wiki/File:Banshee.jpg
http://thomasnastcartoons.files.wordpress.com/2012/06/the-usual-way-sept-2-1871.jpg
http://commons.wikimedia.org/wiki/File:Ringfort_at_Cabragh_-_geograph.org.uk_-_505171.jpg; copyright 2004 by Pamela Norrington
Chapter 29
http://en.wikipedia.org/wiki/File:Euro_coins_and_banknotes.jpg
Thinkstock